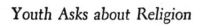

Youth Asks about Religion

YOUTH ASKS ABOUT RELIGION

by

JACK FINEGAN

A Haddam House Book

ASSOCIATION PRESS   NEW YORK

YOUTH ASKS ABOUT RELIGION

Copyright © 1949 by
National Board of Young Men's Christian Associations

Association Press, 291 Broadway, New York 7, N.Y.

Eighth printing, May, 1959

Printed in the United States

PREFACE §∞

ONE DAY a Freshman with whom I was previously un-
acquainted rode with me in my automobile for the short
distance between the campus and downtown. As soon as
he learned that I was a minister, his face brightened and
he said: "I like to talk with ministers. There are two questions I always ask them—What is your definition of God?
and, Do you believe in the soul?" That was a heavy assign-
ment for a ten-minute automobile ride!

The inquiries which students make in regard to religion
are specially penetrating and numerous because they have
to wrestle constantly with the facts and implications of
science, philosophy, and history. Therefore the problems
to which student queries point are also of concern to
thoughtful people in far wider circles, and it is to all of
these—college students, employed young people, and others
both younger and older—to whom this book is addressed.

The questions are such as I have often been asked in
classroom, church, and home, in conference and conven-
tion, in groups and by individuals. The answers also are
what I have given on these many occasions. I have never
tried to give a final pronouncement, but only to reply
frankly and honestly, in the light of my present state of
knowledge and faith, to frank and honest inquiries.

The ideas have been forged in the kind of environment
already described, where the forces of science, philosophy,
and history are powerfully felt. The central intent has
been to try to see the universe whole, and at the same time
to endeavor with all earnestness to comprehend the distinctive meaning of Christianity and its dynamic power.

The approach is my own, and yet I believe it is also

5

in general harmony with a major trend in present Christian thought. On the other hand, there certainly are Christian thinkers who hold very different points of view, and who would give very different answers to the questions. There are occasional references to some of these other ways of looking at the matters discussed. Furthermore, in order to give additional intimation of the many-sidedness of present-day thought and to encourage the continuation of study without which further reaches of truth cannot be attained, some suggestions are made for more reading on each of the chief topics. Though only a few books can be listed, they will be found to include ones that support entirely different modes of thought, as well as my own approach.

The question-and-answer form of the book corresponds to the actual face-to-face situations in which the materials have been developed, and is retained because it is believed that it makes for interest and concreteness of treatment. The questions, however, are arranged in an order of logical progression and grouped under twelve chief headings, to indicate an underlying structure and development. As in personal conversation, I have endeavored above all to express the ideas as simply and directly as possible.

Appreciation is expressed to students and colleagues, past and present, with whom stimulating discussion has been enjoyed; and to Haddam House and Association Press for their constructive interest in the present manuscript.

Permission is acknowledged from the International Council of Religious Education, Chicago, to quote from the American Standard and the Revised Standard Versions of the Bible. Other acknowledgments appear in footnotes.

JACK FINEGAN

Berkeley, California, 1949.

CONTENTS ෧

THE SPIRIT OF THE QUEST

1. Is It Right to Ask Questions about Religion?

YES, IT is right to ask questions about religion. Jesus spent a great deal of time talking with people who came to him with their inquiries. When they asked captious, hypocritical questions, his answers pierced through their sham, but to every honest interrogation he responded with evident appreciation. Many of his most notable teachings were given in the form of such replies.

Albert Schweitzer has said that ever since his youth he has believed that all religious truth must be such that it stands to reason. He holds, therefore, that Christianity should never ask to be excepted from questions, but should be out in the midst of the battle of ideas, "relying solely on the power of its own inherent truth."

It is true that one early Christian writer declared that he believed a doctrine of the church "because it is absurd to believe." Most modern Christians, however, do not feel that way about it. They believe that God has given us our minds to use as fully as we can to seek for truth. They know that faith often goes beyond reason, but they do not believe that it can properly go in absolute opposition to reason.

Therefore it is right to ask honest questions about religion for the following reasons. First, Christianity itself encourages the pursuit of truth. It is written, "You will know the truth, and the truth will make you free."

Second, modern philosophy has developed by using the

method of critical doubt. The honor of being known as "father of modern philosophy" is generally accorded to Descartes. He resolved to doubt everything until he came to something he could not doubt, and then he built his philosophy upon that.

Third, all the truth that there is must at last be one. What is learned by science, by philosophy, and by religion must finally be in agreement. Every inquiry that opens up any truth in any of these areas is a further step toward that fuller understanding which is the goal of humanity.

2. What Is Faith?

There are several ideas as to what faith is. One of these was alluded to in answering the previous question. Faith is believing something "because it is absurd." According to this, the more incredible something is, the greater is the faith displayed by believing it. We have maintained, however, that this sets faith and reason in opposition to each other and denies any validity to reason. Since God gave us our minds with the intention, surely, that we should make full use of them, this cannot be right.

A second way of conceiving the matter is to say that faith and reason both have their place, but that they deal with different areas. The area with which reason is competent to deal is that of "natural" theology. For example, reason is capable of observing certain facts about the universe, such as its orderliness, and drawing the logical conclusion that there must be a First Cause. But there is a higher realm, which is that of "revealed" theology, and here only faith can operate. In this view, divine revelation is something totally different from any other kind of facts, and therefore can be apprehended only by the special faculty of the soul which is called faith. The trouble with this way of looking at the matter is that it makes an artificial and arbitrary distinction between two parts of God's revelation of himself. Where God reveals himself in nature we may use our minds; where God reveals himself in Christ or in the church we can respond only with faith. But surely there are historical facts about the life of Christ and the history of the church where it is necessary for us to use our minds to understand them and where doing so is an essential part of our response to the divine revelation.

Therefore we are constrained to seek yet some other conception of faith. The view we are in search of must recognize that all of God's truth is one, and that faith and reason are complementary rather than antithetical faculties. It is in harmony with these requirements that we define faith as an attitude of experimental daring, of confident assurance, and of personal trust.

Even in science, faith is necessary in the sense of experimental daring. The scientific method comprises the steps of gathering data, formulating a hypothesis, and testing the hypothesis by experiment. The last part of the process can often be carried out only at risk and peril. For example, in learning about the earth on which we live the ancient scientists observed the fact that the North Star sinks lower in the sky as one goes south, and from this datum they formulated the theory that the earth is round. But that hypothesis did not become a scientific fact until it was tested experimentally. The first major experiment was the voyage of Columbus; a second was that of Magellan. Now faith is this same sort of thing in life, too. It is pushing bravely out into some unknown, it is venturing to live according to beliefs that can only be proved by trying them out at personal risk. It is. from this point of view that Sherwood Eddy has said that faith is not believing something in spite of the evidence, but daring something in spite of the consequences.

Faith is furthermore an attitude of confident assurance. Indeed the one formal definition of it in the New Testament states that "faith is the assurance of things hoped for, the conviction of things not seen." Here we are going beyond the immediate evidence, in our inner conviction of what is right and of what the ultimate outcome of things will be.

Again, faith is an attitude of personal trust. It is a basic belief of Christianity that God is a personal being, and if that is so then any relationship to him must be essentially personal and must involve the commitment of the self.

Finally, in Christianity our faith is in God through Christ. It is in Jesus Christ that we have found what the nature of God is like and from him that we have learned to have the attitude that is called faith.

3. Is It Necessary to Be Certain about Everything to Be a Christian?

No, it is not necessary to be certain about everything to be a Christian. If it were, hardly anyone could be a follower of Christ. Almost everyone has doubts of some kind.

Indeed it is usually only a rather objectionable kind of person who claims to be absolutely certain about everything. The Dean of St. Paul's once said about his friend, "I wish I were as sure of anything as Tom Macaulay is of everything." And another remarked, " I have often pillowed my head upon the cushion of ignorance."

As the modest comments of these truly great men show, it is characteristic of Christianity to engender a spirit not of pride in our own fine knowledge but of humility before the surpassing wonder of things infinitely greater than ourselves. It is true that Christianity makes its message known by preaching, but even this proclamation must be made in humbleness. Albert Schweitzer says, "Beware of preaching the gospel as if it explained everything."

We admit frankly then that it is not possible to be certain about everything. There are areas of doubt and uncertainty in the mind of almost everybody. But almost everybody also has at least some measure of faith. There is something in which he believes and to which he is devoted. The question then seems to be whether we will live by our doubt or by our faith. And here the will enters. We can will to swing the emphasis in our lives away from our doubts and put it upon our faith. The remarkable thing is that if we live by doubt and fear, our fears and doubts will constantly increase; if we live by faith, our faith will itself be increased and strengthened.

Perhaps the finest example to keep in mind is that of the man in the New Testament who said to Jesus, "I believe, help my unbelief!" We all have to say that many times.

4. Is Science the Enemy of Religion?

It must be frankly admitted that science has sometimes acted like an enemy of religion, and also that religion has sometimes behaved as an opponent of science. Probably the two most famous examples of controversy between science and religion were the battles over the Darwinian theory of evolution and over the Copernican theory of the solar system. By long gathering of facts and pondering of their interrelationships, Charles Darwin established the hypothesis that all the varied forms of life on earth, including man, are connected in natural lines of development. Belligerent advocates of science forthwith contended that religion's view of man as a spiritual being, and of his origin as a creation of God, was fully discredited. And belligerent apologists for religion maintained that the new theory of evolution was utterly false since it did not agree with a literal reading of the opening chapters of the book of Genesis. Similarly, at an earlier date there was violent argument between the old and apparently biblical idea that the earth is the center of the universe, and the new hypothesis set forth by Copernicus that the earth revolves about the sun. The Roman Catholic Church was strongly enough entrenched at that time so that it could force Galileo, another scientist who accepted the theory, to recant his position. Indeed it was not until 1822, as Sir William Cecil Dampier says in *A History of Science and Its Relations with Philosophy and Religion*, that "the Sun received the formal sanction of the Papacy to become the centre of the planetary system." [1]

From our present point of view such acrimonious antagonism seems most lamentable. We can only explain it as due to fanaticism on both sides. In actuality, science, far from being an enemy of Christianity, is really an expression of it. It belongs to the essence of Christianity to set the minds of men free from every kind of superstition and fear. It sets their faces dauntlessly into the unknown and against every kind of darkness. From this point of view, John Macmurray has declared that "science, in its own field, is the product of Christianity, and its most adequate expression so far."

Nevertheless, science by itself is inadequate to represent man's total response to his universe. With all the unparalleled achievements of science in recent years, our civilization is even now in the direst peril it has ever known. One

---

[1] Third ed., 1942, p. 124. Quoted by permission of the publishers, The Macmillan Company, New York.

philosopher of civilization after another has analyzed the crisis of our time, and all have arrived at essentially the same conclusion—that material development has outstripped spiritual development, and that what we now desperately need is to combine our technical ability with such moral and spiritual discipline that the products of our laboratories and factories shall be used for human welfare rather than for human destruction. This means that henceforth science and religion must work together as friends and allies—or else we shall all perish.

5. Does Everyone Have a Philosophy of Life?

Yes, it seems probable that everyone has at least some kind of philosophy of life. A philosophy of life is really just an idea of what it is all about, and even primitive man had some such idea. As a matter of fact even primitive man often thought about some of the ultimate questions, such as about the Power upon which we are dependent, and about what lies beyond death. Certainly children also ask questions about the meaning of things. Perhaps this spirit of eager interest is part of what Jesus meant when he said that unless we become like children we will never enter the kingdom of heaven. Such a spirit may tend to evaporate as we become preoccupied with things and settle into a habitual routine of life, but most of us have the interests which can lead to the building of a philosophy of life. Almost everyone has some idea of what is worthwhile and of what he is trying to get. This is a part of what it means to have a philosophy of life.

Not everyone, however, has a philosophy of life which he has really thought through and in which all the things that he knows and believes are fitted together harmoniously. Nor does everyone have a good philosophy of life, in the sense that it is a dynamic and inspiring force guiding him increasingly in the achievement of goals that seem to him worthwhile.

What can we do to develop a satisfactory philosophy of life?

First, keep alive the sense of wonder. An ancient Greek epigram declares, "The sense of wonder is and was the stimulus which made men begin to be philosophers." A man who spent a number of years in prison tells that every morning the inmates were taken out for a walk in the courtyard. This area was surrounded by a high and solid wall, and at first he experienced an almost overpowering desire to see beyond it. Sometimes he could hardly keep from breaking out of the line and rushing to scale the wall. His wish was not at all to accomplish an escape, but simply to see what was on the other side. As time went on, however, he gradually lost this impulse and became content to pace up and down with the others on the inside. In life, the maintenance of a fresh interest in what lies beyond the obvious and the commonplace is important if a vigorous philosophy of life is to be attained.

Second, try always to aim for some goal. Man's ability to choose between what is less valuable and what is more valuable is one of his most significant faculties. Like every other ability, it can be dulled by misuse, but can be strengthened by practice. The constant attempt to discover what is truly worthwhile and the constant endeavor to establish a relationship between the activities of life and the ends of life are essential parts of the building of a living philosophy.

Third, hold your present philosophy with conviction, yet with tentativeness. A vigorous commitment to the way of life one holds to be good is necessary; yet a willingness to accept new facts as they become available and to revise one's philosophy in accordance with them is also required. Thus a philosophy of life can be not a static but a dynamic thing, growing and expanding as one progresses.

6. What Is Theology?

Philosophy means literally "the love of wisdom." Thus it comprises the whole quest for truth. In actuality it is a comprehensive undertaking which aims to scrutinize the grounds of knowledge and to synthesize the findings from all fields of investigation in a total view of the world.

What then is theology, and where does it find a place in the adventure of human thought? Etymologically the term means a "word about God" or "systematic truth about the divine." This suggests that theology is a more specialized endeavor than philosophy, and so indeed it is. Just as geology is the science of the earth, and biology the science of life, so theology, by the strict signification of the term, is the science of God. But inasmuch as God is commonly understood to be the ground of all being, theology's very specialization is at the same time a commitment to a truly infinite area of investigation.

In practice, theology usually limits itself to some particular religious tradition. Thus we may speak of Hindu theology, or of Jewish theology, or of Christian theology. In each case the endeavor is to explore and elucidate as fully as possible the system of truth adhered to in that faith. This is clearly necessary if the full contribution of any historic faith is to be adequately set forth to the world. Nevertheless, inasmuch as the deity of Hinduism, the deity of Judaism, and the deity of Christianity must ultimately be one and the same God, theology may, in the prosecution of its task, properly look beyond the limits of any single faith. Thus again we come to the conclusion

that the very nature of the specialization undertaken by
theology leads to the widest possible ramifications.

Theology, then, is a concentrated investigation of man's
understanding of God, particularly as attained in a given
religious tradition. Far from being a narrow undertaking,
however, its scope is of the broadest, since its object of
concern is usually conceived as infinite. Since God is also
the highest possible object of human thought, this investigation is naturally conducted with a special feeling of
solemnity and awe.

7. Should I Be a "Fundamentalist" or a "Liberal"?

It is a good thing to be a Fundamentalist because that
means believing in the fundamentals of religious faith. In
any realm of life, the foundations are very important. In
science, a few basic principles were discovered after long
labor and experimentation. Then later scientists, basing
their work upon these principles, proceeded much more
rapidly and surely. So in religion, the way to make progress
is not to throw away the heritage of the past but to con-
serve and build upon its fundamental truths.

It is a bad thing to be a Fundamentalist, however, when
this means a blind and fanatical adherence to outmoded
forms. There is a story in the Bible about identifying men
by seeing whether they could pronounce the word "Shib-
boleth" correctly. Sometimes Fundamentalism has been
little more than the repeating of a few shibboleths of the
past. When this is the case, religion becomes irrelevant to
the times. The words it utters are those which conveyed a
great meaning in an earlier age. In a new era, to repeat
them without offering any interpretation or explanation in
terms of contemporary thought is almost like speaking in a
foreign language.

It is a good thing, therefore, to be a Liberal because a

Liberal is one who is not confined and bound within the limits of a pattern inherited from the past. Liberalism characteristically seeks to state the truths of religion in the terms of the thought-life of its time. It desires that faith shall be meaningful and effective in each new day. It is receptive to any new light that may come from any source.

It is a bad thing to be a Liberal, however, when this means casting away all that has come from the past. A true scientist, as we have noticed, does not do this. The experimentation of the ages provides the foundation upon which he builds in the present. Furthermore, the very attempt of Liberalism to be modern and up-to-date may mean that it is guilty of excessive accommodation to the spirit of the age. In this case the result is impotence. The process of adjustment has gone so far that the teachings of religion have become indistinguishable from the average set of ideas already held by the common man. Therefore, religion no longer has power to transform and elevate.

Since both Fundamentalism and Liberalism have their strong points and their weaknesses, it would seem desirable for us not to make an advance identification of ourselves with either position. How would it be if we called ourselves Realists, meaning that we want to find and live by all the truth that is available anywhere, whether handed down by the priceless heritage of the past or discovered at the growing edge of contemporary experience? Indeed, since any label can be used as a libel, perhaps it would be better not to try to wear any tag at all, but only to seek to know the truth.

8. *Is Skepticism Dangerous?*

Skepticism means systematic doubt. Descartes, to whom reference has already been made as the "father of modern philosophy," was the most famous proponent of this method. He said that everything was to be doubted. It was his purpose to apply the sharp knife of doubt to all the inherited traditions and beliefs which formed, to his mind, a mass of incongruous opinions. Only by ruthlessly rejecting all sham and falsehood could the way be cleared to attain true knowledge.

It is well known that as Descartes practiced this method, he came at last upon something which he could not doubt. A famous phrase in which he formulated his discovery was, "I think, therefore I am." In his own quaint language he described hypothetical situations where, despite all manner of doubting and being deceived, he still is unshakably certain of his own existence. "I had the persuasion that there was absolutely nothing in the world, that there was no sky, no earth, neither minds, nor bodies; was I not, therefore, at the same time persuaded that I did not exist? Far from it; I assuredly existed, since I was persuaded. But there is I know not what being, who is possessed at once of the highest power and the deepest cunning, who is constantly employing all his ingenuity in deceiving me. Doubtless, then, I exist, since I am deceived, and let him deceive me as he may, he can never bring it about that I am nothing, so long as I shall be conscious that I am something."

As illustrated in the foregoing and as opposed to dogmatism, skepticism is a good thing and a necessary method in the pursuit of truth. Unfortunately, however, skepticism sometimes means not a method of systematic doubt, aimed at constructive ends, but a conclusion already arrived at that any real knowledge is impossible. A symptom of the existence of this kind of skepticism is the habit of suspended judgment. In many cases, of course, while one is seeking for the truth, it is necessary to wait about making up one's mind, but this practice can become a pernicious habit. It is possible to arrive at the point where we are never convinced about anything and never committed to anything. Once I heard an address which was entitled, "The Great God Yes and No." The speaker declared that this was the deity really worshiped on many college campuses and in many fraternities and sororities. With a little taste of scientific method and with some absorption of the spirit of negative skepticism, the first result is often that one says both yes and no to every proposition with which he is confronted. Thus, in the end he believes nothing and does nothing. It is in that sense that skepticism is dangerous.

Let us then use skepticism as a way of beginning the search for truth, but let us not end up in a cynical belief that there is no meaning in anything. Rather let us say with Robert Browning,

> This world's no blot for us,
> Nor blank; it means intensely, and means good;
> To find its meaning is my meat and drink.

9. What Is Truth?

"What is truth?" is a famous question. It was uttered by Pilate at the trial of Jesus. Was Pilate an honest seeker hoping to find by inquiry of Jesus what he had never yet succeeded in finding for himself? Or was he a representative of the negative skepticism which we spoke about in the preceding section? Was he a sophisticated and cynical man of the world who had already made up his mind that it was impossible to find any real meaning in existence? The latter is perhaps the more probable and seems indicated by the way in which the question is introduced in the Fourth Gospel. If that is the case, then despite his power and high position, what a pathetic figure Pilate is. How wretched and fundamentally unhappy he appears in comparison with the Prisoner who stands in his court. The Prisoner has known the truth, has testified to it in his life and work, and is about to bear witness to it by his death. In him, there is no bitter disillusionment, no frustration and futilitarianism, but calmness and peace and radiance. There is no doubt which of the two types of character and attitude represented in that memorable scene appears preferable to us. We can choose which we will regard as our ideal and which we will strive, in our own measure, to be like.

Philosophically speaking, truth might be defined as correspondence between our ideas and the reality around us. This would hold good for truth in the realm of science, for a theory cannot be accepted as correct unless it agrees with the way things behave when an actual experiment is carried out. If an idea is demonstrated to be out of harmony with the way things really are, it must be false. The importance of getting the truth is then clear. Truth represents a knowledge of the structure of reality within which we have to live. Obviously, our life cannot be satisfactory if it is based upon an incorrect notion of the very framework within which it is set. No one can lead a pleasant existence who constantly denies and disobeys the law of gravity!

Similarly in the moral realm, truth is an apprehension of that structure of reality within which we have to make our choices. If we misapprehend the nature of right and wrong in the universe, we will tend continually to make wrong choices and come to unhappy results.

Once again, in the realm of religion, truth is an understanding of spiritual reality. Here, too, we will miss the highest possibilities of life if we fail to find the truth.

Indeed, if spiritual realities are basic in the universe, then truth in this realm is most of all important. Only by finding the truth can we find life.

For Further Reading

Harold A. Bosley, *The Quest for Religious Certainty*. Chicago, Willett, Clark and Company, 1939.

William C. Dampier, *A History of Science and Its Relations with Philosophy and Religion*. New York, The Macmillan Company, 3d ed. 1942.

Hoxie N. Fairchild, *Toward Belief*. New York, The Macmillan Company, 1935.

Hornell Hart, *Skeptic's Quest*. New York, The Macmillan Company, 1938.

C. E. Raven, *Science, Religion and the Future*. New York, The Macmillan Company, 1943.

2

EXPLORING THE UNIVERSE

10. Are We Living in a Cosmos or a Chaos?

THE WORD cosmos has an interesting background. It was originally a Greek noun and was spelled in that language just about as it is in English. The Greeks used it as a designation for the universe as an orderly system. This noun was formed in turn from a Greek verb which meant to arrange or adorn. This is the same root from which we get the word cosmetics. Therefore, cosmetics and the cosmos are related! Cosmetics are that with which a lady arranges and adorns herself; the cosmos is the whole universe as an orderly and beautiful system.

The word which is opposite to cosmos is chaos. This, too, is from the Greek. The Greek word chaos designated the antecedent state out of which the world was made, the unformed mass out of which order came. Thus, this word indicates a situation of confusion and disorderliness.

Now the question is whether we live in a cosmic or a chaotic world. As we look about us, we perceive order on every hand and therefore properly designate our universe as a cosmos. This is true in the area of the large and also of the small. Basing our language again upon the Greek, it is customary to refer to the macrocosm and the microcosm. The macrocosm is the great world, the whole astronomical universe. The microcosm is the little world, the miniature universe which some see in man and others see in the realm of the molecules or the atoms. In the vast world with which astronomy deals, there is order and regularity. Thus, it was possible for Newton, in 1686, to formulate just three laws of motion which described accurately the revolutions of the heavenly bodies. So precise is their regularity that it is possible for astronomers to calculate the reappearance of comets and the occurrence of eclipses many centuries in advance. Similarly, in the tiny world of the molecules and atoms, even if the basis is statistical averages, the regularities are such that chemistry and physics operate in terms of law just as astronomy does. Indeed, it is the fundamental assumption of all science that we do live in an orderly universe. The laws of science do not create this patternfulness. They simply describe it and in a sense reflect it. If we did not live in a cosmos, the entire scientific enterprise would collapse. Indeed, it could never have arisen at all.

Yet one is inclined to ask, What about all the chaotic and disorderly events in the world? What about the tidal waves, earthquakes, and hurricanes which have taken place? What about disease and accident? Well, scientists are grappling with these things on the same assumption that the universe is orderly throughout. Even a hurricane is not a happening outside the realm of order. If we are not yet able to predict it, that is due to the imperfect state of our meteorology. Likewise, in the realm of medical science we do not believe that certain germs are unpredictable in their behavior, but only that we have not yet learned what they are and how to control them. Precisely because all of these things operate within a framework of patternfulness, there is hope for man's eventual understanding of them and conquest over them. Yet we must admit that the more we understand, the more we are aware of what we do not understand. Why, in an orderly universe, should so many things seem to be at cross purposes? No one has ever found a very satisfactory answer to the question of "evil,"

and in one form or another it is about the realest thing we
know. Perhaps the best we can say is that the world is a
mixture of the orderly and the chaotic. The great philosopher, John Dewey, calls it the mixture of the predictable
and the precarious. We may as well accept it as being that
kind of world.

11. What Is the Universe?

The universe is a cosmos. That is plain. But if we probe
more deeply and ask for some kind of an explanation of all
its orderliness, what can we say?

One proposed explanation is that the orderliness has
come by chance. According to this hypothesis, the universe
is made up of a very large number of atoms which are in
wild and disorderly collision with one another. As a result
of an infinite number of such collisions, they bounced into
the formations in which we now observe them. These
formations have the symmetries we described in the foregoing section, but these are purely fortuitous. All things,
including man himself, are, in the famous phrase of Bertrand Russell, "but the outcome of accidental collocations
of atoms."

Several illustrations have been invented to make the
hypothetical process just described seem plausible. In one
of these, we are asked to picture bucketfuls of letters of the
alphabet being tossed ceaselessly into the air. It is supposed
that if this were continued long enough, all of the plays
of Shakespeare would fall down. Another illustration imagines six monkeys strumming unintelligently on type-
writers for millions of years. Here again it is supposed that
if the monkeys only continued long enough, they would be
bound to write all the books in the British Museum.
Actually, all such illustrations seem to render impossible

our serious acceptance of the first explanation of the universe.

A second theoretical explanation of the nature of the universe likens it to a great machine. The solar system can be represented by a mechanical model, and a planetarium can project by mechanical means the motions of the farther heavenly bodies. Thus, it seems reasonable to employ mechanistic terms to explain the universe. The difficulty with this hypothesis is sometimes overlooked. It lies in the fact that every machine introduced as an analogy was itself made by some man or men. There is nothing creative in the mechanical principle. To judge from all that we know anything about, something new is made only as a result of thought. An intricate watch represents the thought and skill of a watchmaker. How much more intricate is the vast universe and how much less possible is it to think that calling it a machine explains its existence.

We seem driven then toward a third way of answering the fundamental inquiry as to the nature of the universe. This third way was suggested a number of years ago when Sir James Jeans remarked, "The universe is beginning to look more like a great thought than like a great machine." As far as we have any opportunity to observe, it is thought alone which is creative. The vast creation which is all about us and which includes ourselves, must therefore be the expression of thought. If this is so, then it seems thoroughly reasonable to go on and say that the thought is that of a Great Thinker and that he is God.

12. Why Is the World Beautiful?

This is a question which, strangely enough, is not often asked. Everybody is aware that the world is beautiful, but it does not usually seem necessary to propound any interrogations about it. Men go and look at the ocean or the Grand Canyon and enjoy it; artists paint and draw and sketch; but not so often is the philosophical significance of beauty in the world made plain to us.

Why is the world beautiful? Why is it not overwhelmingly ugly? A good many times when man gets through with it, it has been turned into ugliness. Man's billboards and slums, his refuse heaps and junk yards, are often what blight an otherwise beautiful vista. Why is it that the colors of an autumn forest or a tropical sunset, even though most gorgeous, are always in harmony? Why is it that a single snowflake under the microscope, or a soaring snow peak filling the whole horizon, are both things of beauty?

Someone, of course, might argue that things are not really beautiful, that it is just in the mind of man that they seem to be. Professor A. Campbell Garnett has answered this difficulty in his book, *God in Us*, by pointing out that regardless of whether it is nature that is wonderfully adapted to have this effect upon the mind or the mind that is wonderfully adapted to receive this effect from nature, in either case the adaptation is equally marvelous.

Now why is there all this preponderance of beauty in the world? Can it be that it is the result of chance? Scarcely, for we have already seen the impossibility of supposing that chance can account for order. How much less could it guarantee the emergence of beauty. As a matter of fact, purely random activity seldom produces anything but ugliness.

Again it might be argued that beauty has a survival value. To a certain extent, this may be true, as when for example, the bright colors of flowers help to attract the bees which are necessary for their pollenization. But there are vast areas of the universe where beauty has no survival value at all, and yet there it is.

We are driven to conclude then that there is some long range influence at work in the universe which is opposed to ugliness and in favor of beauty. Only thus can we reasonably explain the great preponderance throughout the entire universe of the beautiful over the ugly. There must be something at the very heart of the universe which loves beauty and is itself beautiful. As the philosopher Lotze said: "It is of high value to look upon beauty, not as a stranger in the world, not as a casual aspect afforded by some phenomena under accidental conditions, but as the fortunate revelation of that principle which permeates all reality with its living activity."

13. Do the Heavens Show God's Handiwork?

How vast is the universe? With the unaided eye it is possible to discern from 5,000 to 7,000 stars, only half of them of course being visible in our half of the sky. With the one-hundred-inch telescope on Mount Wilson about 1,500 million can be seen. With the two-hundred-inch mirror on Palomar Mountain the light of additional billions of stars, now invisible, will be caught, and man will see twice as far out into space as before.

In measuring distances among the stars it is customary to employ the "light year." One light year is the distance light travels in that time. Since the speed of light is 186,000 miles per second, or about 11,000,000 miles a minute, a light year represents a distance of approximately six trillion miles.

When we look up at what we call the Milky Way we are in reality gazing out through the reaches of the galaxy or island universe of which our solar system is an infinitesimal part. This galaxy is composed of some 100,000,000,000 stars, and it is something like 50,000 light years from our earth to its central point, and 100,000 light years from the earth to its outer edge. Beyond, a million light years away, is another island universe, and on out in yet more remote space are perhaps 100,000,000 other galaxies. One, the distance of which has been measured, is 8,000,000 light years away.

What shall we think as we gaze into the stellar vastness? Sometimes we are inclined to feel that what lies out there is none of our concern, and that for all practical purposes the advice which Albert Einstein once gave an inquisitive questioner is good. The interrogator, who had heard vaguely of Einstein's theory that space is limited in extent, asked, "What lies outside the bounds of the known universe?" "Do not worry," replied the great mathematician, "you do not go out there."

Again, as man has looked into this environing immensity, he has been stirred with the emotion of fear. It was Pascal who cried, "The eternal silence of these boundless spaces affrights me."

But at other times man, gazing up, has been moved to the most exalted considerations, to thoughts of immortality and of God. In a sonnet on immortality, Blanco White imagines primitive man's first experience of nightfall. Did he not tremble, as the sun's light faded, for what was befalling "this glorious canopy of light and blue"? But when the sun withdrew,

> Hesperus with the host of heaven came,
> And lo, creation widened in man's view.

"Why do we then shun death with anxious strife," the poet asks; "If light can thus deceive, wherefore not Life?"

Indeed it is sometimes unsophisticated man, rather than we moderns preoccupied with ourselves and our machines, who is able intuitively to penetrate to the meaning of things. When Lawrence of Arabia told Auda that western man was making better and better telescopes and seeing more and more stars, the Arab sheik replied, "If the end of wisdom is to add star to star without knowing him who is behind the stars, then the Arab way [of contemplation] suits me better." And out in the Congo the saying is heard, "The stars are the lights which he has left burning upon the dark road that leads up to his city."

So it is with faith we may affirm in the words of the Psalmist:

> The heavens declare the glory of God;
> And the firmament showeth his handiwork.

14. Is Life an Accident?

Is the existence of life in the universe a purely accidental happening? The concatenation of circumstances which makes it possible is certainly remarkable. Consider the following facts:

In the stellar universe, of which we have been speaking, some of the stars are hot and shining, others cold and non-luminous. The shining stars have surface temperatures ranging from 3,000 to 30,000 degrees centigrade, and interior temperatures reaching 30,000,000 to 100,000,000 degrees centigrade; the non-luminous bodies have temperatures close to absolute zero, or minus 273 degrees centigrade. In such tremendous heat and utter cold, life as we know it is not possible. Therefore a planetary system is necessary before conditions can be sought where life is possible. But a planetary system probably comes into existence only when two stars pass close together but do not collide. Then, if one of the stars is in the right stage of development, a tide of matter may be raised which comes free from the star and begins to circle around it, eventually coalescing into planets. But so immensely far apart are the stars that, by astronomical estimate, there is likely to be but one system of planets formed in our entire galaxy in 6,000 million years.

In a planetary system, furthermore, a very special combination of circumstances must be found before life is possible. Temperature must stay for the most part between the boiling point of water, 100 degrees centigrade, on the one hand, and a point not too far below freezing, 0 degrees centigrade, on the other. This is an almost inconceivably narrow band of variation compared with the enormous extremes in the universe as a whole. There must be an atmosphere, containing freely available oxygen. There must be water. Such conditions do prevail on this earth, and have done so for something like 2,000 million years. In all that time the range between the maximum and minimum temperatures on the entire surface of the earth has probably not been more than 150 degrees centigrade. But if there is only one chance of the development of a planetary system in 6,000 million years, then, it has been estimated, there can hardly be more than one chance in six million million years that a planet will be produced which provides the conditions of life. And the chance must be still far less that these conditions will remain stable for a billion years. As Ellsworth Huntington says in *Mainsprings of Civilization*, "To say, then, that an earth fit for civilization is a rarity is certainly no exaggeration."

The existence of life, and of man, and of civilization, is then *either* an accident of an almost incredible kind, or it is a manifestation of some great purpose. If it takes faith to believe the latter, the faith required is still not so fantastic as that we would have to display to believe the former.

For Further Reading

A. Campbell Garnett, *God in Us.* Chicago, Willett, Clark and Company, 1945.

Ellsworth Huntington, *Mainsprings of Civilization.* New York, John Wiley and Sons, Inc., 1945.

James Jeans, *The Mysterious Universe.* New York, The Macmillan Company, 1930.

J. Glover Johnson, *Highroads of the Universe.* New York, Charles Scribner's Sons, 1944.

John A. O'Brien, *Truths Men Live By.* New York, The Macmillan Company, 5th rev. ed. 1948.

3

UNDERSTANDING EVOLUTION AND HISTORY

15. When Was Man Created?

IN THE third century A.D., Julius Africanus wrote a work on chronography in which he placed the creation of Adam in the year 5500 B.C. Reasoning by analogy with the Biblical account of creation, he believed that the total duration of the world was to be six "days" of 1,000 years each. This entire period would end 500 years after the birth of Christ, and then would ensue a "sabbath" of 1,000 years. It is obvious that these figures were calculated to fit in with a scheme which was essentially arbitrary.

Similarly Archbishop Ussher, in the seventeenth century, attempted to arrive at a symmetrical chronological system. He placed the date of creation in 4004 B.C., exactly four "days" of 1,000 years each before the birth of Christ in 4 B.C. Two of these "days" he believed to have comprised the period without the Law, and two of them to have constituted the period under the Old Law of Judaism. With the birth of Christ the period of the New Law was inaugurated, and since this period was expected to last for two more 1,000-year "days," the Second Coming of Christ was anticipated for A.D. 1996.

If the relevant chronological notations in the Hebrew Bible are arranged in a consecutive order and added, they total some 153 years more than the 4,004 years which Ussher wished to get, and so he had to allow himself certain rectifications. Furthermore he should have put the call of Abraham in 2004 B.C., but this also did not quite work out.

Another scholar of the seventeenth century, John Lightfoot, made the even more refined calculation that the creation of Adam took place on the morning of Friday, September 17, at 9:00 A.M.

Since these attempts to date the creation were all honest efforts, within the presuppositions of their times, they should not be ridiculed, but they cannot be held as binding upon us, even though they have often found a place within printed editions of the Bible. They were controlled by the prevalent desire for schematization, and they failed to realize that the Bible contains many different documents and does not always profess to give a consecutive and literal chronology.

If we ask the same question as to the date of the creation of man in the light of modern science, we get a staggering answer. The earth itself is over 2,000 million years old. Sometime within the last million years, ape-like mammals developed, or changed suddenly, into man. The oldest skeletal remains which we can identify as possibly human are those of the Java Ape Man from 500,000 years ago. Perhaps 100,000 years ago appeared the Neanderthal Man, who was of the modern genus or race of man; and 50,000 years ago came the Cro-Magnon Man, who was of the same species, Homo sapiens, which today inhabits the earth.

Can what has just been said be reconciled with Genesis? Yes! On the one hand, it may well be that the author of the account of creation in the book of Genesis did not himself mean his words to be regarded as a literal but rather as a poetic account of the origin of man. On the other hand, scientific investigation is dangerously apt to emphasize nothing but the undoubted kinship of man with the natural and animal world, and to be blind to, and unable to deal with, the equally indubitable higher reaches of man's life. Therefore, while we must naturally accept the assured findings of science, we also have great need to keep on reading, pondering, and believing the statement of Genesis: "And the Lord God formed man of the dust of the ground, and breathed into his nostrils the breath of life; and man became a living soul."

16. Is There Room for Freedom in an Orderly Universe?

According to the book of Genesis, freedom entered the picture of life on earth along with man himself. In the plant and animal creation, there was no freedom. The plants grew and the animals roamed the earth in accordance with the necessary laws of their nature. But when man was created, God set definite alternatives before him and endowed him with the ability of choosing between them. The story which tells this is of course narrated in the simple terms of primitive life. The choice which man makes is between fruits of trees in the garden in which he lives. God grants him permission to eat of the fruit of every tree in the garden save one, namely the tree of the knowledge of good and evil. Of that, he is not to eat. Nevertheless, in the exercise of his freedom of choice, man transgresses the Divine prohibition, eats of the forbidden tree, and is punished by expulsion from the garden of Paradise.

This ancient story would seem to be a profoundly true parable. Throughout the entire realm of living things up as far as man, there is no significant freedom of choice. The growth of plants is governed by the laws of their nature, and the behavior of animals is ruled by the instincts implanted within them. These instincts are often extremely wonderful, as when they guide a waterfowl across thousands of miles of trackless land and sea to his destination. But only when we come to man do we find a being who is consciously aware of his ability either to follow his instincts or else in certain situations to go quite contrary to them, suppressing his natural desire in the light of some higher moral purpose. This level of moral freedom is indeed something new and distinctive in comparison with all the earlier and lower levels of life in the universe.

But does moral freedom really exist, or is it just a delusion? Does not the entire universe operate according to law and order? If so, how can there be any freedom anywhere, for would not freedom be a breaking out of the pattern of order and law? Let us grapple with this question by imagining the opposite kind of universe, one in which there was no law and order. In such a universe, everything would happen at random. Nothing would be dependable. Things would behave one way today and a different way tomorrow. Today fire would burn, tomorrow it would freeze. Today the law of gravity would operate, tomorrow it would not. Today stealing would prove detrimental to society, tomorrow, beneficial. In such a world, how could man ever learn to make any choices whatsoever? The only way in which the faculty of moral freedom can be developed is by exercise. If every time man makes the same choice he gets a different result, each contradictory of the last, he can never learn whether he is choosing right or wrong. The only way in which he can possibly develop the power of wise choice and the ability to formulate a long range moral purpose is for him to deal with things that behave dependably. Then gradually and perhaps even painfully, but surely and truly, he can learn by the results whether he is making choices that are essentially in harmony with the structure of reality or contrary to it. Thus, it would seem that to live in a dependable universe is an essential condition for the exercise of moral freedom.

In *Skeptic's Search for God*, Barbara Spofford Morgan makes a distinction between causality and purpose. Causality is the chain of events which lead out of the past to the present. Purpose is the effect of the future already felt in the present. It is the vision by which we shape events toward a yet unattained goal. It is the glory of man that while he lives in a realm of causality, he is capable of shaping his life by purposes that reach into the far future.

17. Is Life on Earth a Jungle Struggle?

In making his choices, man ought to do things which fit in with the main line of development in the universe. The popular conception of evolution seems to be that what has taken place through thousands of years on earth is a tremendous jungle struggle, in which ruthless might has triumphed. Therefore, man should make himself aggressive, brutal, and compassionless in order that he may survive and triumph.

The only difficulty with this picture of things is that it is not true, even to the life of the jungle. Everyone is familiar with the appearance of the ancient dinosaurs as drawn by those who have closely studied their skeletal remains. These animals were enormous, armor-plated monsters. With small brains and colossal bodies, they were perfect embodiments of the popular idea of how to live successfully in this world. At the same time, small, soft-skinned animals which we call mammals already existed. In comparison with an eighty-ton dinosaur, they were utterly weak and helpless. Yet they were marked by proportionately greater brain power and by more attention to their young. In the outcome of things, the dinosaurs perished and the mammals prevailed.

Evolution is, therefore, not a blind jungle struggle but a process in which the qualities of intelligence and co-operation lead to success. The apparently imponderable qualities of thought and love have more to do with survival than the obvious attributes of size and strength.

The same thing can be illustrated, it would seem, in the history of nations. In the ancient world there was no more ruthless nation than Assyria. This impression is based largely upon the inscriptions of the Assyrian kings themselves. Perhaps they were boastful and exaggerated. Nevertheless, the things of which they speak are significant of their interests. Again and again in their inscriptions, they tell of their cruelties in war, how many cities they stormed and sacked, how many princes they flayed, how many heads they cut off, how much blood they shed. This nation whose boast was in its military cruelty rose with meteoric swiftness and brilliance to world dominion and then it plummeted with unparalleled swiftness into oblivion. Its once proud capitals were forgotten heaps of sand until our own time.

In the same days when Assyria was bestriding the earth with its unrestrained power, there was another nation which was tiny and weak. This was the Hebrew people. Many of them were deported and much of their land was despoiled by Assyria. The Assyrian nation perished but the Hebrew people lived on and ultimately made their imperishable contribution to the religion of the world.

It would seem clear then that there is something to the long process of evolution and history on earth which will not let blind, cruel might have the last word. To choose to live in such a way is not to be in harmony with the main drive of the universe. To fit in with the main direction of things, we need to develop along the lines of thought, co-operation, and righteousness.

18. What Does Calamity Do to Society?

It is a pleasant picture if we can believe that intelligence, co-operation, and righteousness lead to success, but what about all the calamities that there are? The book of Revelation tells about four horsemen who ride forth across the earth. The first horseman is on a white horse and carries the bow of war. The second rides a red steed and has the sword of revolution. The third is seated on a black horse and holds a pair of scales signifying famine. The fourth bestrides a horse of pale, corpse-like color which stands for pestilence. War, revolution, famine, and pestilence, these are the four horsemen of the Apocalypse who ride so often and with such terrible results across the face of the earth. What can intelligence, co-operation, and righteousness avail against them?

Well, it is precisely against such enemies as these that intelligence, co-operation, and righteousness are our chief weapons. It is in the darkness of ignorance, fear, and superstition, it is in the absence of mutually helpful association, and it is for the lack of the basic qualities of righteousness that war, revolution, famine, and pestilence prevail on earth. The only way to attack these things is by scientific research, wider education, and more general understanding; by joining individuals and nations in associations of peaceful co-operation; and by spreading the fundamental principles of morality all around the world.

It will of course be a long time before all of these calamities are banished from the earth. In the meanwhile, what do they do to society when they strike? Professor Pitirim A. Sorokin has written an important study of this very question under the title, *Man and Society in Calamity*. He says, in essence, that calamity is a tremendous driving force in human history. Some people remain about the same under its impact, many are driven into disintegration, while others are impelled to some of the sublimest achievements that have ever been known in the history of the world. Some of man's most important inventions have been made, some of his greatest books written, and some of his most saintly and self-sacrificing acts performed under the pressure of calamity. What makes the difference between those who go to pieces and those who rise to great heights in such a time? Professor Sorokin says that it is largely a matter of whether they have a well-integrated system of values or not and whether they are looking chiefly toward the city of man or the kingdom of God. Those who have a real pattern of values, of things which they believe in and live for, and those who are devoted not solely to material things but to spiritual ends are able to bear the blows of calamity and to translate these into impulsions to higher levels of living.

Therefore, our fundamental analysis seems substantiated. It is by devotion to the processes of thought, the patterns of co-operation, and the principles of righteousness that we best put ourselves in line with the main drive of the universe and are best able to survive the disastrous blows which fall.

19. What Is the Goal of Evolution?

According to the second law of thermodynamics, the universe is slowly running down like a great clock. Vast amounts of energy are steadily being transferred into heat which is dissipated throughout space. The tendency is for all bodies to come at last to the same final temperature. This process of the degradation of energy appears to be irreversible. At each successive stage, there is less available energy than before. The eventual outcome, it would seem, can be nothing other than a dead universe. Is this the goal of evolution?

The foregoing statement refers to the realm of inorganic evolution. When we turn to the area of organic evolution, a somewhat analogous state of affairs seems to be implied by the Darwinian theory as commonly understood. A major emphasis is there placed upon adaptation to environment, but when a perfect adaptation to environment has taken place, the result would appear to be the achievement of a state of stagnation. An example is the sandworms which have existed now practically without a change for hundreds of millions of years. Is this the goal of evolution?

In his notable book, *Human Destiny*, Lecomte du Noüy points out that the really significant fact about evolution is that things are not running down into a state of universal stagnation. In many cases, such as that of the sandworms, this is of course true. But again and again in other cases, some new form will appear and a step will be taken toward a higher level of life. Thus, instead of getting a state of perfect equilibrium and eternal stagnation, what we really find in evolution is a drive manifesting itself in a multitude of ways and breaking out, as it were, from time to time in totally unexpected transformations.

If this is what evolution really is, then its goal, so far as discernible by us, must be that end toward which these successive transformations appear to tend. What sort of end is that? The first part of the process is physical and appears to have fairly well reached its goal. Man enjoys the benefits of an erect posture, an opposed thumb and forefinger, stereoscopic vision, and a relatively large brain. These physical endowments are of crucial importance for the exercise of man's dominion over the rest of creation as promised in Genesis. But the second part of the process has only begun. By virtue of his higher faculties, man lives in a realm of philosophical, moral, and religious values. By what he does in this realm, man is able self-consciously to influence the process of evolution, either retarding it with willful wrong-doing or accelerating it with purposive endeavor. The highest visible goal of evolution is, therefore, the spiritual perfecting of man, a goal in the attainment of which man himself now has a large degree of responsibility.

For Further Reading

Robert Calhoun, *What Is Man?* New York, Association Press, 1939.

Humphrey J. T. Johnson, *The Bible and Early Man*. New York, The Declan X. McMullen Company, Inc., 1948.

Barbara S. Morgan, *Skeptic's Search for God*. New York, Harper and Brothers, 1947.

Lecomte du Noüy, *Human Destiny*. New York, Longmans, Green and Company, Inc., 1947.

Pitirim A. Sorokin, *Man and Society in Calamity*. New York, E. P. Dutton and Company, Inc., 1942.

Arnold J. Toynbee, *A Study of History*. Abridgement by D. C. Somervell. New York and London, Oxford University Press, 1947.

4

GOD

20. *Is It Intellectually Respectable to Believe in God?*

IT SEEMS to be statistically respectable to believe in God. A Gallup poll, conducted in eleven nations, gave figures for belief in God ranging from sixty-six per cent of the population in France to ninety-six per cent in Brazil. In the United States, so the poll reported, ninety-four per cent of the people express a belief in the Deity.

It is also historically respectable to believe in God. Many of the greatest philosophers from Plato to Kant to Whitehead have devoted much of their thought to God. Many of the greatest scientists, likewise, have been firm believers in God. The names of men like Tycho Brahe, Francis Bacon, and Newton come immediately to mind. Furthermore, as Robert A. Millikan reported with statistical documentation in his book, *Time, Matter and Values,* among the "distinguished scientists" of today, more of the younger than of the older men report themselves to be believers in God.

But none of us can decide a matter like this on the basis of statistics alone, or just by being told what certain other people think about it. We must ask for ourselves whether belief in God squares with our best possible understanding of the universe. To that question it seems possible to give an affirmative answer. As we have explored the universe and sought to understand evolution and history, the patternfulness of the world and the purposiveness of evolution have come unmistakably before us. It does not make intellectual sense to reduce all of this to "chance." So little, indeed, does that make sense that even some who try to speak with complete scientific objectivity and impartiality have been driven to invent the term "anti-chance" to explain this great tendency which works through all things. But if it is intellectually respectable to believe in "anti-chance" then it is at least not less so to believe in God as the Creator of this orderly world and the Establisher of those purposes which drive toward far-off spiritual goals.

21. Is God Anthropomorphic?

Anthropomorphic is an English word made out of two Greek roots. The first, *anthropos*, was the Greek word for man, and it appears also in such modern terms as anthropology. The second Greek root is *morphe*, meaning form, which also occurs in an English word like morphology. Anthropomorphic means, therefore, in form like a man, and particularly refers to the representation or conception of God as being in human shape and with human attributes and emotions.

There is no doubt that in the third and eleventh chapters of Genesis, for example, whether they are intended literally or poetically, the representation of God is in anthropomorphic terms. In the first case, we have the story of the Garden of Eden and are told that the Lord God was "walking in the garden in the cool of the day." In the second case, we have the story of the Tower of Babel and are told that the Lord "came down to see the city and tower, which the children of men builded."

Now let us suppose that we want to avoid anthropomorphism. What shall we do? As Professor Streeter once pointed out, what modern man most often does is to fall into "mechanomorphism." Obsessed with his clever machines and impressed by the mechanical aspects of the universe, he thinks of God in mechanical terms. He envisions the universe as a vast machine and conceives total reality as existing in the form of a machine. Others who would no longer use the machine analogy so crudely still think of God in terms of impersonal law and process.

But this will hardly do! Here we are, personal individuals contemplating God and reducing him to something less than ourselves. Personality is self-conscious and purposive. These attributes apply neither to a machine nor to a law. Therefore, on the foregoing hypothesis, we are reduced to the absurdity of maintaining that a mechanistic, impersonal process has eventuated in the emergence of self-conscious, purposive personality.

It seems better, therefore, to take the position that personality is not only the highest fact within the realm of our experience, but also the best clue to the nature of ultimate reality. Since persons exist and are able to think, experience beauty, and strive after the right, there must be at the heart of the universe a personal reality whose values are likewise those of truth, beauty, and goodness. This can be called anthropomorphism if one will, but it is assuredly a spiritual anthropomorphism. Indeed, it must be said that anthropomorphism has commonly been a mark of vitality in religion. A spiritual anthropomorphism which conceives the highest reaches of man's life as having an essential kinship with what is deepest in the nature of the universe is not only a vital but also a logically defensible position. It accords with the profound biblical insight which declares that "God created man in his own image, in the image of God created he him."

22. *Is God the Sum Total of Human Ideals?*

In the Scriptural reference just cited we saw how the Bible states that God created man in his own image. In modern times it has become fashionable among some thinkers to declare that exactly the reverse is true, that actually man created God in his own image. The line of reasoning here employed runs to the effect that God is obviously an idea cherished by the human mind. Man conceives the thought that there is a Supreme Being and naturally pictures this Supreme Being as like himself. Indeed, a rationalistic explanation of the idea of God somewhat of this sort was given as long ago as the sixth century B.C. when Xenophanes declared that if oxen, lions, and horses were to carve images, they would fashion gods after their own shapes and make them bodies like to their own. The highest form of this kind of explanation appears in our day in the humanistic affirmation that God is only the sum total of human ideals. Man takes his highest hopes and purposes and projects them against a cosmic background. That is his God. The sooner we recognize that God is not really there, and adjust ourselves to working toward our own otherwise unsupported ideals, the sooner we will understand what life is really like in this universe. Such is the argument.

What is wrong with that? Only one thing is wrong with it, namely, that it changes God from an objective into a subjective reality. Now there is no need to deny that God is subjectively apprehended by us. That simply means that the only way we can know him is in our minds and through ideas and experiences that are a part of our own human life. But this is far from saying that God has no existence save as an idea and an ideal in our minds. It has been characteristic of every great religion to believe that God is an objective reality. If there is any being whose existence is derived and illusory, it is man himself. According to Hinduism, man is caught in a net of illusion and can only escape by recognizing the essential identity of his soul with the Soul of the universe. In the Old Testament, God is described as "from everlasting to everlasting," and man as being "like grass which groweth up—in the morning it flourisheth, and groweth up; in the evening it is cut down, and withereth." Surely, the very heart is taken out of real religion if its central faith is destroyed, namely that man is a created, dependent being, whose Maker and Sustainer is one infinitely greater than himself. Similarly, the lines of scientific observation and philosophical reasoning which we have essayed in the foregoing sections all converge toward the conclusion that the universe is only intelligible as the result of a great purpose. If this is true, then in his highest strivings man is not vainly endeavoring to lift himself by his own bootstraps, but is relating himself in conscious dependence to that mighty force not himself which makes for righteousness.

23. What Is Your Definition of God?

There is a bewildering variety of definitions of God. Some are skeptical, and declare that he is the Unknowable (Herbert Spencer), or explain that he is an Illusion, born of the need to make tolerable the helplessness of man and built out of the material offered by memories of the helplessness of his own childhood and the childhood of the race (Sigmund Freud). Some are humanistic, and call him the Common Will of Humanity (H. A. Overstreet), the Symbol of Highest Social Values (E. S. Ames), or the Imagined Synthesis of Ideal Ends (John Dewey). Some are naturalistic, and identify him as the Principle of Concretion (A. N. Whitehead), or as that Order of Existence and Possibility by virtue of which the greatest possible good is truly a possibility and can be achieved by human effort (H. N. Wieman). Some are descriptive of an emerging deity, and say that he is a Growing God (William James), or the Spiritual Nisus of an evolving universe (C. L. Morgan). Some picture him as finite, and state that he is a conscious Person of Perfect Good Will limited by the free choices of other persons and by restrictions within his own nature (E. S. Brightman), or an Eternal Cosmic Mind who suffers when matter makes his plans miscarry (J. E. Boodin). Some use the analogy of a particular aspect of man's mental processes and call God the Cosmic Mathematician (Sir James Jeans), and others decline to use any human comparison whatsoever, and call God the Utterly Other (Karl Barth). A Biblical definition, found in John 4:24, is the concise statement, "God is a Spirit." In the common usage of the word, "spirit" is that which is capable of living, thinking, willing and loving. Thus God is a personal Being who lives, thinks, wills, and loves, and who is the universal source of life, thought, righteous purpose and noble love.

In philosophical thought about religion it seems necessary to try to define God. Yet, having formulated the best definition of which our minds are capable, we are reminded of the French saying, *Dieu défini est Dieu fini*. With a play on words that can hardly be reproduced in English, this sentence declares that God defined is God finished. The infinite greatness of God cannot be brought within the compass of a small definition; if it be so confined it is lost. Hence, beyond all our definitions we would retain a sense of wonder and amazement at that which exceeds the bounds of our comprehension.

24. What Varieties of Belief in God Are There?

There are, as this question suggests, many varieties of belief in God. In order to describe and classify them, a series of technical terms has been devised. The basic root in the formation of these terms is derived from the Greek word *theos*, meaning God. To the root is added the suffix *-ism*, signifying belief or doctrine. Thus *theism*, etymologically, connotes belief in God in general. To this word, various prefixes are joined to specify particular kinds of faith. The first prefix is the letter *a-*, which serves as a sort of minus sign, and gives the word *atheism*, meaning belief that there is no God. Next comes *polytheism*, which means belief in many gods. Since there are many forces at work in nature man early conceived the existence of numerous deities to account for these manifestations. Such belief in a multiplicity of divine beings has continued to characterize many living religions. *Katheno-theism* is the tendency within polytheism to give the supreme place to one god for a time, and then to another, one after the other. *Henotheism* is belief in one god, though not to the theoretical exclusion of the existence of others. *Monotheism* is belief in only one God. It is often customary to use the word *theism* to connote belief in one personal God. *Panentheism* is the doctrine that God includes the world as a part of his being, but is not the whole of it. *Theopantheism* is the teaching that God is all, and *pantheism* the almost indistinguishable doctrine that all is God. Such are the ranges of thought about God, from the denial of his existence at one extreme to the affirmation at the other extreme, that all that there is is God. Towering up between is the central faith that there is one supreme, personal being, creator of the world but not identical with it, who is God.

Since discussion often proceeds with terms which are philosophical rather than strictly theological, three other technical words should also be mentioned. These are: *pluralism*, the theory that there are many different principles at work in the universe; *dualism*, the belief that the universe is divided between two mutually opposed elements; and *monism*, the doctrine that there is only one kind of ultimate reality.

25. Who Founded Monotheism?

There is some evidence, which has been collected and discussed chiefly by Wilhelm Schmidt, that points to the existence in the mind of primitive man of belief in one high God. In historical development, however, only three great religions have attained to a strong and consistent monotheism. These are Judaism, Christianity, and Islam. It is noteworthy that all three emerged from a Semitic background in the ancient Near East, and that each grew in a real way out of its predecessor or predecessors. Since Islam was dependent upon both Christianity and Judaism, and Christianity came out of Judaism, it is evident that we must look to the Jewish faith for the first emergence of monotheism.

It is commonly held that it was the Hebrew prophets of the eighth and later centuries B.C. who originated the doctrine of one God. The theory is that prior to that time the Israelites had worshiped a tribal or national god, who was only one among many such deities believed in by the various peoples of the ancient world. Amidst the international problems of their time, the prophets perceived that there was only one ethical principle and one moral law to which all nations were subservient, and hence they concluded that there must be only one God over all the peoples. Isaiah 45:14 declares unequivocally, "Surely God is in thee, and there is none else, there is no (other) God."

The maintenance of this hypothesis of a relatively late invention of monotheism runs into two difficulties. The first is the fact that the prophets of whom we have just been speaking did not present their teaching of monotheism as an innovation, but rather as a summons to return to something which their people had long believed but had often sadly failed to live up to. The second fact is the extremely interesting circumstance that long before, in the fourteenth century B.C., down in the land of Egypt an Egyptian king named Akhnaton had expressed faith in one universal God. This we know from the discovery of hymns, carved in tombs at Tell el-Amarna, which were composed by him and his associates, in which the sun-god, Aton, is called the "sole God, beside whom there is no other," and is described as creating the world, setting each man in his place, and supplying all with their necessities.

Actually, the traditions of the Old Testament point not to the later prophets but back to an earlier figure, Moses, as the founder of monotheism. Moses must have led the children of Israel out of Egypt either around 1441 B.C. or more probably around 1290 B.C. Thus he lived either a little before or a little after Akhnaton, whose dates are approximately 1377 to 1360 B.C. Moses worshiped God under the name of Yahweh, or Jehovah, to use the less correct spelling with which we are more familiar. The etymology of this name probably indicates that Yahweh was considered the Creator of All. As believed in by Moses, Yahweh was considered to stand alone, to be restricted to no special abode, and, although anthropomorphic in at least his feelings and sympathies, to be beyond representation by any image or idol.

The founding of monotheism thus goes back at least to the time of Moses. Professor William F. Albright, one of the world's most eminent students of the ancient Near East, says, "If . . . the term 'monotheist' means one who teaches the existence of only one God, the creator of everything, the source of justice, who is equally powerful in Egypt, in the desert, and in Palestine, . . . who is human in form but cannot be seen by human eye and cannot be represented in any form," [1] then Moses, the founder of Yahwism, was certainly a monotheist.

26. Is God Interested in Human Individuals?

In space and time man is almost utterly insignificant. In a universe the dimensions of which are measured in millions of light-years, the earth is a hardly noticeable speck of dust. Yet this is the only home man has. Furthermore, it is but a small part of the total surface of this speck of dust that is actually occupied by man. The whole human race could be put into a cubical box one mile on each side and this could be swallowed up by that single crack in the earth's surface which we call the Grand Canyon. If the total two billion inhabitants of the earth constitute a no more impressive mass than this, how diminutive must any single individual seem.

Similarly, when measured against universal time, the existence of man seems extremely brief. Speaking of the earth alone, its total age may be two billion years. The modern genus of man first appeared about 100,000 years ago. That makes the whole life of the human race occupy only the last 1/20,000th part of the age of the earth. As for the Christian Era, it fills only the last one-millionth part

---

[1] From *The Stone Age to Christianity* (1940), p. 207. Quoted by permission of the publishers, The Johns Hopkins Press, Baltimore.

of the earth's age. Again, if we think of the life-span of an individual man, it is a yet more infinitesimal fraction of cosmic time.

Such figures as these often produce what someone has called "astronomical intimidation." There is perhaps no better reply than the other remark that "astronomically speaking, man is the astronomer." Throughout all the vast reaches of space and time of which we have just been speaking, there is nowhere an awareness of it all, as far as we know, save in the mind of man. If we were to ask for one of the largest things in the universe, we might think of the star Betelgeuse, which has a diameter three hundred times that of our sun. But what is it? An enormous mass of incandescent gas which man measures. As an illustration of a long enduring thing, we might recall a great redwood tree that has had a living existence of over two thousand years. But it knows not itself and only man brings to it an awareness that combines scientific calculation concerning it with esthetic appreciation of its majesty and beauty.

What would God be interested in in all of his vast universe? Only in things which have large size or which last a long time? Will he not be concerned with those beings which, apparently tiny and transitory as they are, are endowed with "god-like" gifts of self-awareness, thought, and appreciation?

Although the Bible was written prior to the period of modern scientific discovery, it reveals a keen sense of the relative insignificance and the ephemeral quality of man's life. The insignificance of man is described in the eighth Psalm:

> When I consider thy heavens, the work of thy fingers,
> The moon and the stars which thou hast ordained;
> What is man, that thou art mindful of him?
> And the son of man, that thou visitest him?

But the Bible also gives us precisely the insight for which we have been striving. The eighth Psalm continues immediately:

> For thou hast made him but little lower than God,
> And crownest him with glory and honor.

This is the dignity of man. He is endowed with attributes which are related to those of God himself. It is the Christian faith that God is concerned about man, every single human individual.

27. How Can One Believe in God When There Is So Much Evil in the World?

This is perhaps the oldest and most stubborn problem of all and it may even be insoluble from our limited point of view. Nevertheless, it seems necessary to seek at least the best answer we can to the question. This has been sought along the lines both of reason and of faith.

Intellectual considerations direct attention to the following facts: First, a great deal of what seems evil to us is simply the work of an orderly universe. The behavior of the universe, as described by the laws of science, is faithful and regular. The law of gravity is not suspended in order to save a man from harm when he falls off a roof. It may be that the *man* is disorderly! The suspension might cause an amount of damage to other persons far outweighing the benefit to this man. Furthermore, we would never really learn to be "orderly" about falls if the law of gravity were constantly being nullified in emergencies. The existence of law in the universe sometimes seems to work for our harm, but it could not really be otherwise if we are to learn to live.

In the second place, a great deal of evil certainly comes

because man has the power of free choice. In exercising his power of freedom, he often chooses what is wrong. These wrong choices bring disaster and suffering.

In the third place, man lives in a social solidarity. He is intimately interconnected with his fellows throughout the whole web of society. Indeed, in our day these interconnections ramify until they extend all around the world. Thus it is that the ignorant act or wrong deed of some person may have far-reaching effects. The consequences of the act may fall upon those who are utterly innocent.

These three facts seem at least partially to explain some of the evils in the world. Evils come because of our ignorance of the laws of the universe and of life, because of our perverse and sinful choices in the face of the great alternatives of right and wrong, and because of the interconnectedness of society which allows the baleful effects of wrongdoing to spread out over ever-widening circles and down through successive generations. These explanations may not be fully satisfying, yet we should remember that the very same conditions that open the way for evil also open the way for all learning, moral development, and human progress. If we did not confront an orderly universe we could never develop any reliable understanding of life. If we did not face genuine alternatives of right and wrong, we could never grow in moral stature. If we did not live together in a society, we could not share the benefits of the insights and achievements of others. Therefore, evil, black and terrible as it is, need not drive us to the doubt and denial of God. It is evident that we live in the kind of world where it is possible to *combat* evil, and we may believe that he desires to help us to do so.

It is not likely that a thoughtful person who has seen or felt pain will be satisfied by any intellectual explanation of its place in the world. In the midst of severe personal suffering—his own or someone else's—he cannot stop to "reason" it out. Then it is that he needs *faith* that "underneath are the everlasting arms." In the presence of pain and humiliation and defeat one can still feel himself a part of something larger than himself that sustains and comforts him, and strengthens him to put forth every ounce of energy to correct wrong and change evil to good, believing that the effort is worthwhile.

28. Can God Do Anything He Wishes?

It has been customary in Christian theology to declare that God is omnipotent and omniscient—all-powerful and all-wise. Surely most Christians regard the object of their worship as possessing these exalted attributes. God, then, must be able to do anything he wishes. But the matter is not quite so simple as that.

For one thing, there are certain limitations implicit in the very nature of a perfectly wise and good being. If it is his thought which establishes the eternal principles of wisdom, then he cannot go contrary to those very principles. He cannot make something true which is false, or false which is true. He cannot make a circle square, or cause two plus two to equal other than four.

Again, there are limitations which are set up by the very fashion in which God has created the universe. If he ordains that its behavior be in accordance with the laws of motion and of gravitation, then he cannot be expected to interfere arbitrarily with that faithful behavior and destroy the pattern which he has himself established. If he inaugurates the vast process of evolution, he must allow it to work toward its goal in accordance with the guiding principles which he has ordained.

Once more, there are limitations due to the nature

which God has bestowed upon man. He has given man the inalienable and precious right of freedom. He will therefore respect that right and will not nullify it by forcing man to do something not freely chosen.

These limitations are logically implicit in the nature of God, the universe, and man. To recognize them is not to impugn the perfection of God, it is to trace some of the outlines of that perfection.

29. Can a Miracle Happen?

According to a materialist a miracle cannot take place. The universe operates according to its laws, and there can be no deviation from them. According to traditional religious belief, on the other hand, any kind of miracle can take place any time, if God wills it to. Which is correct?

The first view, which denies the possibility of any miracle, seems to imprison God within his universe. The second, which thinks miracles may occur at any time, seems to disregard the very structure of reality which we believe represents God's thought and purpose. Therefore neither conception is very satisfying to a thoughtful person. Is it possible to look at the matter from any other point of view?

The following theory defines miracles in three ways, and says frankly that the first kind of "miracle" probably never takes place, but that the other two kinds do. The first type of miraculous happening would be an arbitrary interference with the faithful regularity of the behavior of the universe. It would be an act of God contrary to the laws of his world. The temporary suspension of the law of gravity would be a case in point. There is little evidence that such a "miracle" ever takes place. As far as we know, no authentic example of such an event has been observed, and as far as we can see, such an act on the part of God would be out of harmony with his own nature.

The second type of miracle is a happening that is wonderful to those concerned and quite beyond their own power to accomplish, but it takes place *through* the working of the regular known laws of the universe. It is the working together of the various factors involved, and their convergence upon the particular time, place, and people, that is remarkable and beyond the reach of human power. Many of the miracles in the Bible would seem to fall within this category. If the crossing of the arm of the Red Sea by the children of Israel was made possible by the favorable and concurrent action of tide and wind, and if the falling of the walls of Jericho was due to an earthquake at the time the Israelites came there, then that people surely would thank God for wonderful deliverance and wonderful victory.

The third kind of miracle is an event in which God acts through laws *beyond* those now known to man. There is reason to believe that there are great reaches of the universe and its laws that still lie yet beyond the ken of man. Possibly some of these laws may become better known as man grows in moral and spiritual character, as he progresses in stages of evolution that have as yet barely begun. But God can work through such higher reaches of reality even now, perhaps in answer to the prayers by which men of faith touch realms beyond rational comprehension. The miracles of healing performed by Christ may illustrate the working of such higher laws, some of which are now coming dimly into view in the understanding of man as a "psychosomatic" being whose mind and body intimately affect each other.

That God should actually work in the ways supposed by our second and third types of miracles, to answer prayer and to bring good into human life beyond what man can do, is in harmony both with his own nature and with the essential structure of his universe.

For Further Reading

William F. Albright, *From the Stone Age to Christianity*. Baltimore, The Johns Hopkins Press, 1940.

H. H. Farmer, *God and Men*. Nashville, Abingdon-Cokesbury Press, 1948.

A. Eustace Haydon, *Biography of the Gods*. New York, The Macmillan Company, 1941.

Walter Horton, *God*. New York, Association Press, 1937.

C. S. Lewis, *Miracles*. New York, The Macmillan Company, 1947.

Robert A. Millikan, *Time, Matter, and Values*. Chapel Hill, University of North Carolina Press, 1932.

Margaret L. Runbeck, *The Great Answer*. Boston, Houghton Mifflin Company, 1944.

A. E. Taylor, *Does God Exist?* New York, The Macmillan Company, 1947.

5

JESUS CHRIST

30. Did Jesus Really Live?

THROUGH THE comparative study of religions it has become well known that myth and legend play a part in many faiths. The Mystery Religions, for example, which prevailed widely in the Roman Empire in the first century A.D., were often based upon the mythical experiences of some god or goddess. Osiris, Isis, Horus, Cybele, Demeter, and Mithras, were some of the deities around whom such cults were centered. Was Christianity just another such Mystery Religion with an equally mythical founder? Lewis Browne gives the answer in his book, *This Believing World*, when he is endeavoring to explain why it was that Christianity won the victory in a world that was already so full of other faiths. "Only the Christians," he remarks, "had a real man to worship."

Do we have dependable knowledge of Jesus as an actual historical person? Yes. In the first place we have the testimony of the letters of Paul. This testimony is particularly significant, for two reasons: One is that this man was at first an enemy of Christianity. He would hardly have been persuaded to join this movement if he had known that its founder had never existed, but was only a myth manufactured in men's imaginations. Another reason for giving special importance to what we learn of the historical Jesus in Paul's letters, is the simple fact that this information is so very incidental and casual. The letters were written for the purpose of helping churches and individuals with specific problems and questions. But they indirectly disclose a great many facts about Jesus' life and his character and work. Paul and the other Christians knew them perfectly well, from unimpeachable witnesses, and simply took them for granted.

In the second place we have the evidence of the Synoptic Gospels. These are the first three Gospels, called "synoptic" because they all look at the life of Jesus from the same point of view. As careful, comparative scrutiny discloses, the oldest sources here are the Gospel according to Mark, and a Collection of the Sayings of Jesus, now lost in its original form, but utilized by Matthew and Luke. From the Synoptic Gospels we are enabled to see the life of Jesus in a comprehensive historical context, and to feel the impact of his personality and message.

In the third place we have the witness of the other documents of the New Testament. Most or all of them are later than these we have already mentioned, but even though they are concerned with new problems in the life of the church, and reflect advancing speculation, they contain much important information about Jesus, and clearly show forth the essential character of his life.

Most of these books of the New Testament, upon which we depend for our knowledge about Jesus, were written in the first century A.D. We now have an actual fragment of a copy of one of them, namely the Fourth Gospel, which dates from the first half of the second century A.D., less than fifty years after the original was written; and we have a copy of a collection of the letters of Paul, which dates from the beginning of the third century A.D., only 150 years after Paul wrote the originals. From the fourth century on, we have many other important manuscripts, giving us in all a great body of evidence for the establishment of the text of the New Testament.

Now it is certainly true that all of the many manuscripts and all of the various New Testament documents have to be studied historically and scientifically, but it may be affirmed confidently that they provide us with the strongest kind of evidence for the historical existence of Jesus. Indeed, another great Jewish scholar, Joseph Klausner, declares, "If we had ancient sources like those in the Gospels for the history of Alexander or Caesar, we should not cast any doubt upon them whatsoever."

31. What Facts Can We Be Sure of about His Life?

We cannot be sure of the exact date of the birth of Jesus. One would suppose this date was identical with the beginning of the Christian Era, but actually there was a certain amount of error in the calculation of the beginning point of this Era. The gospels tell us that Jesus was born when Herod was King of the Jews, and we know from secular history that Herod died in 4 B.C. Therefore Jesus must have been born not later than in that year.

We know approximately how old Jesus was when he began his public work. Luke tells us this explicitly: "Jesus, when he began his ministry, was about thirty years of age."

And we know with a good degree of assurance, the date of the crucifixion of Jesus. All of the gospels tell us that this event took place on a Friday, and the Gospel according to John shows that Jesus was crucified at the same time that the Passover Lamb was slain by the Jews for their great annual religious feast. Combining these facts with laboriously calculated astronomical tables and calendars, Professor A. T. Olmstead, in his book, *Jesus in the Light of History*, gives the exact date of the crucifixion as April 7, A.D. 30.

Now something like this same state of affairs prevails with regard to everything about the life of Jesus. The information is relatively scanty for the earlier years; it increases sharply for the period of his actual ministry, and it is fullest of all in regard to the Last Week and the death of Jesus. This is natural, for the early church was concerned most of all with what Jesus did and said in his actual work, and with how he laid down his life for his followers.

Concerning the dependability of our knowledge of these matters, Professor E. F. Scott has remarked, "We need to begin with the great indubitable facts—that Jesus inspired his followers with a boundless devotion, that he brought good tidings to the poor and distressed, that he worked for the kingdom of God and was faithful unto death. These are the foundations of the history, and no criticism can shake them."

32. Is "Christ" a Name or a Title?

Jesus is the name that was given to the founder of Christianity at his birth, as we are told in Matthew 1:21. This name was frequently used among the Jewish people. It is the same as the Old Testament name Joshua, or Jeshua. It has appeared recently on some stone ossuaries of the first century A.D., found in a cave-tomb between Jerusalem and Bethlehem. Here we find that one man, for example, was named Jesus Aloth.

In contrast with the personal name of Jesus, Christ was originally a title. It is the same word in Greek as the word "Messiah" in Hebrew. This word literally means "anointed." The significance of it goes all the way back to ancient times when the Hebrew king was installed in his royal office by the ceremony of anointing. Then, after their political nation was destroyed and they no longer

had a king on the throne at Jerusalem, the Jewish people
hoped very much that sometime in the future God would
raise up a new king for them and restore their national
glory. To this coming King and Deliverer, they naturally
applied the title, the "Anointed One," that is the Messiah,
or the Christ. Around this title, then, all of their hopes
and longings for a better future were gathered. Sometimes
they anticipated that the Messiah would be a literal king,
reigning with a mighty sword at Jerusalem and destroy-
ing all their enemies; again they supposed that he would be
a heavenly Judge, who would pronounce doom upon all
the ungodly; and again, as in the books of Zechariah and
Isaiah, they thought that he would be one who was meek
and lowly, and a suffering servant of mankind.

When Jesus once asked his followers, "Who do men
say that I am?" they reported that the common opinion
was that Jesus was John the Baptist come back to life
again after being slain by Herod Antipas, or that he was
Elijah whose return to earth was expected before the end
of the world, or that he was some other one of the prophets.
When Jesus asked, "But who do you say that I am?" Peter
answered on behalf of the group, "You are the Christ."
They believed he was not simply a prophet, or one of the
forerunners of the kingdom of God, but none other than
the long-hoped-for Messiah who would actually establish
that kingdom.

This has been the faith of the followers of Jesus ever
since, and inasmuch as they are disciples of the "Christ"
they have become known as "Christ-ians." This name was
first applied to them in the city of Antioch, as we are
told in Acts 11:26.

Strictly speaking, then, Jesus was the personal name and
Christ the title of the founder of Christianity. But ap-
propriately and properly enough, men came to refer to

him generally by both of these words at the same time.
Ere long it was almost forgotten that "Christ" was anything but part of a personal name too. Hence we commonly speak of him as Jesus Christ. Paul did this regularly,
and sometimes also reversed the two names and said Christ
Jesus. It is perfectly proper to do this, but it enriches our
understanding if we remember that using the word
"Christ" carries with it the very confession of our faith
in the one who was "anointed" by God to establish his
Kingdom.

33. What Is the Kingdom Which Christ Proclaimed?

According to Mark 1:15, the very first preaching of
Jesus was an announcement of the kingdom of God. This
kingdom was a Jewish hope. The Hebrews started out
with the same idea that was shared by other Semitic peoples
as well, namely, that God was their king. The other
Semitic peoples did not get much further with the idea.
They thought that the god of their tribe was their king.
Therefore, if they were overcome in battle, their king was
also defeated. The god of some other tribe was more
powerful than their own. The Hebrew people attained
a loftier conception of God than that. They believed that
there was only one God over all the nations, and that he
ruled with righteousness. But this seemed to be con-
tradicted by the hard facts of experience. Within their
own nation not everyone was obedient to God, and outside among the heathen there was an arrogant flaunting of
human pride against God. Thus, the Hebrews believed,
the time was yet to come when God would manifest his
power and establish his as yet unseen rule in visible reality.
This strong anticipation enabled the Jewish people to
endure exile and persecution with dauntless faith. In this

form this was originally a strictly Jewish hope, but it is also a universal hope. It corresponds to widespread human longings. Professor E. F. Scott compares it with the belief of the Greek thinkers in a world of pure intelligible forms, the expectation of Augustine and Dante of a holy theocratic state, and the practical thought of our time which strives for a renovated social order. So when Jesus spoke of the kingdom of God he referred to something which his own people greatly longed to see, and when he uttered the sentence, "Thy kingdom come, thy will be done, on earth as it is in heaven," he gave a prayer in which all men everywhere can join.

As Jesus told about the kingdom of God he spoke of it as something which belongs to the future but also as something which is even now present. The prayer we have just quoted asks that the kingdom may come. Certainly, as long as war, slums, crime, drunkenness, race hatred, and starvation exist, the kingdom lies far beyond our present achievement. Yet, on the other hand, the kingdom is in a real sense already present. It is here now in the ceaseless activity of God, and it is present in the mighty deeds of Jesus. "The kingdom of God is in the midst of you," Jesus told his disciples, and to his antagonists he declared, "If it is by the finger of God that I cast out demons, then the kingdom of God has come upon you."

Similarly, the kingdom of God is both something outward and something inward. When it comes it will involve such a rearrangement of society that the abuses which disfigure the present will be eliminated and those perfections of which we dream will be visibly manifest. But we ourselves cannot live a hundred years, or a thousand years, or a million years, waiting for the kingdom to come. Can we then have none of it? Yes, according to the teaching of Jesus, we can possess it inwardly even now.

"The kingdom of God," he declared, according to the alternative translation of Luke 17:21, "is within you." Paul, the great follower and interpreter of Jesus, wrote, "The kingdom of God does not mean food and drink but righteousness and peace and joy in the Holy Spirit."

Once again, the kingdom of God is something very great but also something very simple. Of course it is a great thing because it involves God's rule of this stupendous universe, and the ultimate perfect establishment of his holy will. But the kingdom is also something very simple and close at hand. The Reverend H. R. L. Sheppard has told the story of a great artist who in his old age said that he could remember perfectly the first occasion when he deliberately turned his back on the kingdom of God. He was a schoolboy at the time, home for the holidays, and as he walked down the village street, a small girl to whom he was something of a hero ran out of a cottage and offered him a bunch of rather faded flowers, doubtless the very best she could procure. The boy passed her by without taking the gift. Later, a little ashamed, he looked back and saw the child in tears and the flowers scattered on the road. Dr. Sheppard said: "I believe the offer of the Kingdom is the invitation which Jesus daily gives to you and to me to permit love and not hate to prevail now and here in our life, our work, and our home."

34. What Did Jesus Christ Wish to Accomplish?

Since Jesus accepted the confession of his disciples that he was the Christ, he must have wished to establish the kingdom of God. As we have seen, this kingdom was the first thing of which he spoke as he began his public preaching. Now many people thought that the only way the kingdom of God could be established was by the rise of a military Messiah who would drive the hated Roman oppressors out of the land and re-establish the anciently splendid kingdom of the Jews. Such a kingdom might even be extended to encompass many heathen lands, some of the nationalistic prophets believed. There is good reason for supposing that when the devil showed Jesus all the kingdoms of the world in a moment of time, and offered to give them all to him, it was really a temptation to pursue the militaristic way of conquest and seek the goal of national glory. Jesus refused this way.

Other popular opinion at the time anticipated that the kingdom of God would be established by supernatural intervention. Remembering the visions in the book of Daniel, not a few people looked toward the clouds of heaven and expected to see the Messiah someday seated there, conducting the Last Judgment. The devil also, we remember, suggested to Jesus that he perform supernatural wonders such as casting himself down from the pinnacle of the Temple and having the angels bear him up, and his own disciples are reported in Luke 19:11 to have "supposed that the kingdom of God was to appear immediately," evidently in some such supernatural fashion as corresponded with the popular expectation. But Jesus did not do anything like this.

What then did he wish to accomplish? He wished to establish the kingdom of God, not in the way which corresponded to the superficial anticipations of the multitude, but in the way which fulfilled the will of God himself. This is the reply he made to the insidious temptations of Satan, when he quoted Deuteronomy 6:13, "You shall worship the Lord your God, and him only shall you serve." Therefore he followed the guidance of the Spirit of God in his heart, and walked along a way that led to the Cross, and to the imperishable establishment of a spiritual kingdom in the hearts of men.

35. What Did He Teach?

Instead of founding a military empire or performing supernatural exploits, Jesus Christ "went about . . . teaching" (Matthew 4:23). From one of his own parables we can see how this was an integral and indispensable part of establishing God's kingdom. The parable was the story of the sower who went out to sow. Some of his seed fell on the path and was trodden under foot; some fell on rocky ground and soon withered; some fell among thorns and was choked; and "some fell into good soil and grew, and yielded a hundred fold." While Jesus may have simply left this parable as it stood and expected his disciples to comprehend its meaning, the gospels contain an explicit explanation of it as a setting forth of the secrets of the kingdom of God. The seed is the word of God, planted by Jesus in the field of the world, some of which, received in faithful lives, will grow into the fruits of the kingdom.

What sort of teachings, then, did Jesus give as the creative principles of the kingdom of God? There are many rich and varied things which he said, all of them in their impact being nothing less than tremendous, "gigantesque" words, as E. C. Colwell has said in *An Approach to the Teachings of Jesus*. But when they asked him for the most important truth of all, he responded with a two-fold teaching: "The first is . . . 'You shall love the Lord your God . . .' The second is . . . 'You shall love your neighbor as yourself.'" The teaching of Jesus is therefore in the first instance a profoundly religious teaching. It relates the life of man to the ultimate ground of his existence, and calls upon him to love God completely. In the second instance, and intimately related to the first, it is a dynamically ethical and social teaching. It calls for love of one's fellow man, without any of the limits which were customarily associated with such a teaching in the Old Testament.

The kind of love which Jesus called for is designated in the New Testament by the Greek word *agape*. In the wonderfully precise Greek language there are no less than three words which are all customarily translated by "love" in English. One is *eros*, from which our word "erotic" is derived; another is *philia*, which means friendship; and the third is *agape*. Agape is the distinctive kind of Christian love. Perhaps it is best to define it simply as the kind of attitude and concern which Jesus himself manifested. In relation to God, then, love is an attitude of trust in the heavenly Father; in relation to man, it is compassionate concern and intelligent good will. This is the word which is at the heart of the kingdom of God, and which, planted in the hearts of men, will grow to bring that kingdom.

36. Did Christ Actually Heal People?

As complete a record as we have of a day in the ministry of Christ is that which is found in Mark 1:21–34. This day was spent in Capernaum, a prominent city of New Testament times on the western shore of the Sea of Galilee. This day was the Jewish Sabbath, and Mark's gospel pictures Jesus going into the synagogue and teaching there. In the synagogue, however, was "a man with an unclean spirit," and Jesus made the unclean spirit come out of him. As far as we can tell, the unclean spirit represented a mental malady of some sort, and Jesus healed the man thus afflicted. The next thing we are told in the record of this same day is that Jesus went to the home of Simon and Andrew after leaving the synagogue. There he found that Simon's mother-in-law was sick with a fever, and he healed her of this. The report of these wonderful deeds evidently spread rapidly, for we read further that when evening came, that is when the Jewish Sabbath was over, and free movement and work were possible, a large number of sick and afflicted people were brought to his door. Mark states, "And he healed many who were sick with various diseases, and cast out many demons."

What shall we do with accounts such as these? We may ignore them, because it is hard to give a scientific explanation of them, but that is not too satisfactory. We may endeavor to eliminate them from the records of the life of Christ as stories spun by wonder-loving imaginations. Perhaps some of the stories have been so developed or heightened. There are too many of them, however, throughout all the gospels, and they constitute too often an integral part of the account, to make it possible for us to tear them all out.

Again, we may try to rationalize them. This was done by such early writers on the life of Christ as Herder and Paulus, for example. The typical rationalistic explanation would run something like this: Simon's mother-in-law, for example, had been sick for some time and her fever had run its course. When Jesus came to her home and took her hand and lifted her up, this provided the little extra stimulus to enable her to shake off her lassitude and return to the normal course of life, a thing which she would very shortly have done anyway. This type of explanation, however, makes Jesus virtually an impostor, since he apparently took advantage of such situations to heighten his own fame. As Albert Schweitzer said about rationalism, "The method is doomed to failure because the author only saves his own sincerity at the expense of that of his characters."

The only remaining alternative, then, seems to be to accept the fact that Christ actually performed what we call "miracles" of healing. The philosophical background for understanding such happenings has already been laid in our answer to the question whether miracles can happen. We have there reasoned that there may well be higher laws in the universe other than those with which we are yet familiar. One who is able to work in harmony with those higher laws could accomplish results which would seem nothing less than miraculous. There seems to be a distinct possibility, then, that Jesus was operating in a realm of the mind and spirit where there are wonderful possibilities yet little known and realized by man in general.

One illustration may make this more plain. It may be found in the book, *After Everest*, by T. Howard Somervell. Somervell was a mountaineer who participated in one of the great attempts to climb Mount Everest. After the expedition was over, he traveled in India and saw the unrelieved suffering of that land. Being a doctor, he went there to work as a medical missionary. To the hospital where he was stationed came a man upon whom a leg operation had been performed by an unskilled surgeon. X-rays revealed that the whole bone of the leg was infected from top to bottom with tubercular disease. When told that amputation offered the only chance of saving his life, the man replied unexpectedly, "Will you give me three weeks? I want to try the effect of praying about it." He left the hospital, ill and with a fever, capable only of being carried about. Three weeks later, true to his promise, he returned, this time hobbling with a stick and looking much better. The X-ray showed that the leg was improved, though not yet free from the disease. Three weeks later he came back again, and at that time the leg was found to be healed. A few months later and he was back at his regular work as a teacher in a boys' mission school. The man explained simply that he and his family and friends had joined in a chain of prayer asking for healing. Somervell remarks, "He and his family had proved that the age of miracles is not over. Who can say what contribution India may not make to the religion of the world when she has, like this man and his family, been introduced to God as Christ showed Him?"

We must, however, also remember that so great a saint and servant of Christ as the apostle Paul earnestly besought release from a physical affliction and received not the material healing which he asked but rather the spiritual sustaining indicated by the words, "My grace is sufficient for you." We are not dealing therefore with the practice of magic but with the realm of faith.

37. Why Did Jesus Die?

Many historical factors contributed to the death of Christ. The Roman imperial system constituted one of these. It was organized to preserve law and order. This meant, according to Roman ideas, the unhesitating liquidation of any revolutionaries who imperiled the existing order. The watch for such fomenters of rebellion was particularly sharp in Palestine because that land had been a veritable seed-plot of revolt. When Jesus, therefore, was accused to the Roman procurator as one who pretended to be a king, it became immediately probable that his life would be forfeited.

Another factor was the Jewish religious system. With all of its noble aspects of spiritual insight and ethical imperative, this system had to a considerable extent hardened into a structure of legalism and ritualism. When, therefore, Jesus freely broke prescriptions relating to Sabbath observance and fearlessly drove out of the temple courts those who polluted it with commercialism, he was bound to become the object of bitter antagonism from those whose vested interests were bound up with the religious system as it stood.

The everlasting weaknesses of human nature also played their part in the chain of events which led to the death of Jesus. At one time, the multitudes of people were enthusiastic about him. Again, they were transformed into a mob crying for his death. Among Christ's own disciples, there was one who betrayed him. Whether the traitorous deed of Judas was done out of sheer avarice and disloyalty, or perhaps with the thought of forcing Jesus at last to declare himself as a supernatural king, we do not know. Nevertheless, the deed was done and it contributed its part to the tragic outcome.

It would be possible to enumerate yet other historical forces which converged toward the crucifixion of Christ, but all of these factors together seem insufficient to really explain the death of Jesus. He does not impress us as one who simply died as the unwilling victim of forces which were beyond his control. Rather, one who had meditated profoundly upon the deepest significance of the life of Christ reported his saying about the laying down of his life, "No one takes it from me, but I lay it down of my own accord." That is certainly borne out by the things which Jesus did. When he was warned to flee from Galilee because Herod wanted to kill him, he continued his work without the slightest deviation on account of that threat. When he started to Jerusalem and his own disciples urged him not to go on account of the dangers there, he nevertheless went steadfastly on. When he went to the Garden of Gethsemane to pray, he was doing, Luke tells us, exactly what his regular custom was. There was no slightest attempt to hide or flee. In brief, he took every step with wide-open eyes and clearly formed purpose.

Why then did he die? Because in the will and way of God, this was necessary for the accomplishment of his work. Long before, a prophet of very high spiritual insight had spoken of a suffering servant whose sufferings would have vicarious value for mankind. Jesus made himself a Messiah not of military or spectacular kind, but of the kind envisioned by that ancient prophet. At the Last Supper with his disciples, he himself broke bread to them and passed to them a cup saying, "This is my body which is broken for you. . . . This cup is the new covenant in my blood." That is how he regarded the death he was about to die.

38. Can We Believe in the Resurrection?

We cannot help believing in the resurrection, although we cannot entirely explain it. All of the Gospels contain some records relating to the resurrection. Paul, also, who wrote before any of our Gospels were composed, placed strong emphasis upon the resurrection. Indeed, he said flatly that if Christ has not been raised from the dead, Christian preaching is in vain and Christian faith is in vain. Beyond the testimony of these honorable men, we have the witness of history itself. We know that the disciples were utterly crushed by the crucifixion of Christ. When he was taken captive, they left him and fled. After his death they evidently returned to their old occupations. All of their hopes had gone for nought. Then not long after we find them reassembled, renewed in faith, and restored in courage. Indeed, they have an access of power which they had not had before. Nothing now can stop them. They go across all the world of their day with the message of Jesus Christ.

When we try to explain exactly what happened, we are, to be sure, at a loss. The Gospel records tell many different things. Paul himself speaks as if the resurrection appearances of Christ to his disciples had been of the same kind as the experience which came to himself on the Damascus road. And of that experience, several accounts were current in the early church. Perhaps, at least for the purpose of this brief answer, it is best to content ourselves with recalling the unequivocal assertion of Paul that Christ died for our sins in accordance with the Scriptures, that he was buried, that he was raised on the third day in accordance with the Scriptures, and that he appeared to Cephas, then to the twelve, then to more than five hundred brethren at one time, then to James, then to all the apostles, and last of all, says Paul, "he appeared also to me."

The details of the resurrection and the nature of the spiritual body in which the immortal spirit is clothed are matters which lie beyond human comprehension. But if we are asked whether we believe that the life of Jesus Christ was ended by death and that was all there was to it, or that beyond death he was raised to everlasting spiritual life, that he is a living presence in the world, and that at the end of the world he will be triumphantly vindicated in the kingdom of God which he died to establish, there can be no doubt as to our answer.

For Further Reading

John W. Bowman, *The Religion of Maturity*. Nashville, Abingdon-Cokesbury Press, 1948.

Lewis Browne, *This Believing World*. New York, The Macmillan Company, 1926.

H. J. Cadbury, *Jesus: What Manner of Man?* New York, The Macmillan Company, 1947.

E. C. Colwell, *An Approach to the Teachings of Jesus*. Nashville, Abingdon-Cokesbury Press, 1947.

C. H. Dodd, *The Parables of the Kingdom*. New York, Charles Scribner's Sons, 1936.

C. H. Dodd, *History and the Gospel*. New York, Charles Scribner's Sons, 1938.

Walter M. Horton, *Our Eternal Contemporary*. New York, Harper and Brothers, 1942.

John Knox, *The Man Christ Jesus*. Chicago, Willett, Clark and Company, 1941.

John Knox, *Christ the Lord*. Chicago, Willett, Clark and Company, 1945.

John Knox, *On the Meaning of Christ*. New York, Charles Scribner's Sons, 1947.

Mary Ely Lyman, *Jesus*. New York, Association Press, 1937.

A. T. Olmstead, *Jesus in the Light of History*. New York, Charles Scribner's Sons, 1942.

T. Howard Somervell, *After Everest*. London, Hodder and Stoughton Limited, 1936.

6 ♥

THE BIBLE

39. How Did the Bible Get Its Name?

THE BIBLE got its name by a very interesting chain of circumstances. The chief writing material of the ancient world was papyrus. In its natural state, papyrus was a reed which grew abundantly in the swamps of Egypt. From this reed, thin strips were cut and laid side by side and crosswise to form a relatively light and extremely durable writing material. This was made in sheets and they were pasted side by side and then rolled up into a scroll. Such a scroll was the usual form of a book when the New Testament documents were written. Those documents must have been written on such pieces and rolls of papyrus. The tiny letter to Philemon would probably have occupied no more than a single leaf of papyrus, but the Gospel according to Luke would have filled a roll over thirty feet in length. We must think, then, of the New Testament books as written originally and existing originally in the form of such scrolls.

Papyrus is a Greek word and from it our modern word paper is directly derived. The pith of the papyrus stalk, however, was called *biblos* in Greek, and from this was derived the diminutive form, *biblion*, as the regular term for a papyrus scroll. When, therefore, the early Christians referred to a book like the Gospel according to Luke, they would naturally call it a *biblion*. For all of the New Testament books put together, they would simply use the plural of the same word which was *biblia*. Indeed, to the

81

Christians this was a quite sufficient designation of these documents. They were "*the* scrolls" or "*the* books," of supreme value above all others. So they just called them that. Finally, in Latin the plural noun *biblia* came to be regarded as a singular form, and thus, at long last, our word "Bible" came into being. Naturally enough, the name was applied not only to the New Testament books but also to the Old Testament ones which were conjoined therewith.

40. Why Is There an Old Testament and a New Testament?

Over a period of many centuries, the Jewish people developed a great body of religious writings. Those which were of most value were incorporated in their collection of sacred scriptures. These were written, for the most part, in the Hebrew language and this Hebrew Bible was arranged in three divisions. The first division was called *Torah* or *Law*. It comprised the books from Genesis to Deuteronomy, containing the Law of Moses. The second division was called *Prophets*, and included not only books which told history from a prophetic point of view, like the volumes from Joshua to Kings, but also the works of the great literary prophets from Isaiah to Malachi. The third division was entitled *Writings* and comprised documents of such varied character as Daniel, Psalms, Job, and Ecclesiastes. All together, these three divisions constituted the *canon* or authoritative collection of Hebrew scriptures.

In the centuries immediately preceding the Christian Era, these books and some additional ones which had meanwhile been written and accepted, were translated into the Greek language for the benefit of the many Jews living in the Dispersion.[1] In addition to containing a number of books which were not in the Hebrew canon, the order of the various books was now considerably rearranged. The Hebrew scriptures began with Genesis and ended with Chronicles while the Greek scriptures began with Genesis and ended with Maccabees.

Now, as we well know, Jesus himself was a member of the Jewish people and his first disciples were also Jews. Moreover, out among the Gentile world, many of the first converts to Christianity had previously been Jews. All of these Jewish people, naturally, were familiar with and regularly used the Jewish scriptures which we have just described. The next thing that happened was that various Christian documents, such as the letters of Paul, the four gospels, and other writings, were composed and gradually collected into a body of sacred Christian literature. Christians, therefore, really had two collections of sacred writings. The first was that which had belonged originally to the Jews, the second was that which was composed in the course of the development of Christianity itself.

In both collections, the word "covenant" or "testament" was important. In the older writings, it was told how God had entered into a covenant with Abraham and his descendants. It was felt by the prophets that the Jewish people had been untrue to that covenant and Jeremiah prophesied that in the future a new covenant would be established. In the Christian writings there was the record

---

[1] The "Dispersion" is a technical term that refers to the scattering abroad of the Jews into many countries outside of their homeland. This dispersal was begun by the forcible deportations recorded in the Old Testament but was continued as a result of voluntary emigrations, the seeking-out of business opportunities, and other reasons. Living in lands where Greek was spoken, these scattered Jews naturally adopted it as their own language too.

of how Jesus, on the night in which he was betrayed, had eaten a Last Supper with his disciples and had given them a cup which he said was the covenant in his blood. Therefore, the death of Christ constituted the ratification of the new covenant between God and man. Inasmuch then as the older collection of books comprised the record of the first divine-human agreement, it could properly be called the Old Testament; inasmuch as the newer collection contained the ratification of the new agreement between God and man, it could properly be called the New Testament. Thus it is that our entire Bible is composed of these two main parts so designated.

41. Did the Biblical History Truly Take Place?

A great deal of the Bible is occupied with telling us things that are supposed to have taken place during past centuries. The writers of the Bible seemed to feel that it was chiefly through these events that God became known to man. In other words, the religion of the Bible is essentially a historical religion. Therefore, it is quite important to inquire whether the events that are narrated in the Bible really transpired or not.

To get a thoroughgoing answer to this question, it is of course necessary to work through the entire Bible and deal with every portion and every narrative individually and separately. Although this cannot be done here, we can at least give some indication of the general result of such study. If we begin our investigation with the patriarchal narratives, that is those concerning Abraham, Isaac, and Jacob, the forefathers of the Hebrew people, we find that these stories, although they must have been handed down orally for centuries, fit in very well with what is now becoming known through archeological research of ancient

life, laws, and customs in upper Mesopotamia. If we consider the Exodus, we find that it is possible to identify
some of the sites in Egypt and in the peninsula of Sinai
where the children of Israel are said to have been. Also,
as we have already seen, we find that Moses, the founder
of Hebrew monotheism, lived not far from the time of
a great Egyptian king who also formulated a monotheistic
belief. The general setting is such that the emergence at
that time of the children of Israel into a more unified
people devoted to the worship of Jehovah is thoroughly
credible.

If we follow the children of Israel in the conquest of the
Promised Land, we find through actual archeological ex-
cavation in Palestine that many Canaanite cities suffered
destruction at just about the time the Israelites are supposed to have come. Also, at about this time, we find the
Israelites mentioned on an Egyptian monument as a
people actually in Palestine. When we advance to the
time of Solomon, we are able to point to an excavated city
in Palestine which was probably one of his chariot cities,
and to a seaport city at the head of the Gulf of Aqabah
where the same king conducted extensive manufacturing
and commercial activities. In the case of yet later kings, we
find their actual names appearing on contemporary Assyrian
and Babylonian monuments.

As for New Testament times, it is possible in Palestine
to identify many of the sites and ways connected with the
life of Christ. Also, out in the Mediterranean world, not a
few similar identifications are possible with respect to the
travels of Paul. For a single example, in telling of Paul's
work at Thessalonica, Acts 17:6 calls the city authorities
at that place "politarchs." [1] This word is otherwise un-

---

[1] See the *New Translation* by James Moffatt.

known in all Greek literature, but the very word was actually found in an inscription on a Roman arch still standing in modern times at that city.

By putting together a great many such observations, we arrive at the general conclusion that certainly in its broad outlines, and many times even in its small details, the Biblical history truly took place.

42. Does the Bible Agree with Modern Science?

We have already noticed in discussing the relations of science and religion that some people who have accepted science wholeheartedly have, as an apparently necessary consequence, attacked the Bible vigorously for its lack of agreement with modern scientific conceptions. On the other hand, there are some valiant defenders of the Bible who with equal vigor maintain that the ideas and achievements of modern science are already foreshadowed in the Bible. To give a single example of the latter mode of thought, we may notice an interpretation of Nahum 2:4. This passage reads as follows: "The chariots shall rage in the streets, they shall jostle one against another in the broad ways: they shall seem like torches, they shall run like the lightnings." What the prophet Nahum actually was referring to was the battle in which the great city of Nineveh was destroyed in 612 B.C. The kind of interpretation with which we are now dealing, however, supposes that he was looking into the twentieth century A.D. and giving a precise description of modern automobiles! Do they not run like lightning, do they not have headlights like torches, above all, do they not constantly have collisions on Broadway?

The view which seems preferable to either of these extreme positions is that the Bible is not primarily concerned with the kind of problems to which science devotes most of its attention. The Bible is concerned with religion and with the historical and personal experiences in which men felt themselves touched by the purpose of God. In connection with the worship of God, the Bible refers to the overwhelming impression of majesty and awesomeness made by the starry heavens. It is concerned with the religious implications of this fact, not with the computation of the distance to a given star. Both of these matters are proper objects of concern. The two modes of thought, the two ways of outreach of the human mind and spirit, are not in antagonism to each other; rather, they are complementary the one to the other. In setting forth its religious message, the Bible, of course, often reflects the scientific views which prevailed at the time it was written. Sometimes these are surprisingly like our own. An example is in the first chapter of Genesis where the progression of events in the Creation runs from the making of the inanimate universe to the creation of animals, and last of all of man. This is a general order of events, not unlike that envisioned by the present theory of evolution. Nevertheless, the main principle of interpretation must remain a recognition of the historical origins of the Biblical documents and of their primary religious purpose.

43. Were the Writers of the Bible Inspired?

"All scripture," we are told in II Timothy 3:16, "is inspired by God and profitable for teaching, for reproof, for correction, and for training in righteousness." That is a plain statement of high regard for the Scriptures as truly inspired by God. When II Timothy was written, the documents of the New Testament had not yet been collected or even all written, therefore the reference must have been to the Old Testament Scriptures; nevertheless, as the New Testament writings were similarly brought together into a recognized canon, the text may justly be interpreted as applying in its essential import to the entire Bible.

What does it mean to call the Biblical writings inspired? To help answer this question, we may recall a statement in II Peter 1:21. Here in relation to the origin of the Scriptures, it is said, "Men moved by the Holy Spirit spoke from God," or according to the reading of some ancient manuscripts, "Moved by the Holy Spirit, holy men of God spoke." The Bible is inspired, we may take it from this passage, because the men who wrote it were inspired. This must mean that they were men of such character and devotion that the Spirit of God could influence them in their thinking and writing.

If what has just been said is correct, then believing in the inspiration of the Bible does not mean arguing that every syllable of it is a direct and infallible utterance of God. We may freely recognize the full part played by the human agents. They were fallible human beings, necessarily men of their times, and of course limited in various ways. If they reflect scientific views, moral standards, and religious insights characteristic of their time, that is precisely what is to be expected. Nevertheless, through them a word is being spoken that progressively gains in clearness and power and is really and truly the Word of God.

44. What Philosophy of History Is Presented in the Bible?

The Bible seems to be the first book in the world in which a great philosophy of history is worked out. The Oriental religions, broadly speaking, were little interested in history, because they often regarded human existence

as an illusion from which it was desirable to escape. The
Greeks and Romans generally believed that things went
around in circles, and thus there was little chance to formulate a conception of a linear development in history.
Most of the writers of the Bible, however, believed that
God had a forward-looking purpose for his people in their
historical existence. In trying to trace out the meaning of
this purpose and to get their people to follow it, these
writers worked out what may properly be called a philosophy of history.

One of the formulations of this philosophy may be
observed in the Old Testament book of Judges. The stories
collected in this book concern the men who were the
leaders of the children of Israel after their entry into
Palestine and before they first had a king. The connotation
of the name "Judge" includes the idea of establishing
justice. To do this, evil must be put down and righteousness made to prevail. The Judges, therefore, were not
simply men who sat on a bench and handed down legal
decisions. They were active protagonists of their people's
cause in stormy times. Actually, the stories about the
Judges are among the most vigorous and sometimes blood-
thirsty of any in the Bible. They can hardly stand up
against the standards of later Christian times, although the
things they describe are not worse than things done in
modern wars.

The editor who collected these accounts of the exploits
of the Judges saw the events of that time falling into a
definite pattern. This pattern of events had four phases.
The first phase was the apostasy of the children of Israel.
Pledged though they were to the service of Jehovah, they
would fall away into the worship of other gods. Along with
that would come a lowering of moral standards and a
weakening of the common life. The second step inevitably

was destruction. Their enemies, the many surrounding
heathen nations, would triumph over them. The third step,
then, was repentance. In their desperate need, the people
would remember God and cry out to him again for help.
This led to the fourth phase in the cycle of events, namely,
deliverance. God would raise up one of the Judges. This
man or woman would contend valiantly on behalf of his
people, cast down their enemies, and re-establish the
security and welfare of the land. Thus, the four phases
through which history passed were those of decline, defeat,
contrition, and salvation. The fact that the people passed
through this cycle many times, only shows, as the adage
has it, that we learn from history that we learn nothing
from history. Nevertheless, the writer of this book believed that there was a pattern in history, and that by
setting it forth clearly it would be possible for his people
to learn from history, and to order their national life in
accordance with that far-reaching purpose of God through
which alone they could make true progress. The schematization of events which he set forth may be an over-
simplification of history. Nevertheless, it was an earnest
attempt to read the meaning of historical existence and
it affirmed that there is a moral law running through history.

45. What Work Did the Prophets Do?

The prophets did a great deal of the actual work of
forging the view of history referred to in the preceding
section, and of bringing it to bear constructively upon
the life of the Hebrew nation. The great prophets, from
Amos on, lived in a world of international affairs. The
small land of Palestine lay between the mighty homes of
empire in the valley of the Nile and the valley of the

Tigris and Euphrates rivers. On the one side was Egypt, on the other side were Assyria, Chaldea, and Persia. Amidst the shifting alliances and intermittent wars of the time, the kingdoms of Israel and Judah were constantly tempted to pursue a course of intrigue and to play in the dangerous game of power politics.

At home, likewise, there were mounting problems. The commercialization of life, the increase of wealth and luxury on the one hand, and the steadily deepening misery and degradation of the poor on the other, were marks of the contemporary situation.

It was in this world of international war and national decay that the prophets of the Bible did their work. This was to attempt to discern and interpret the purposes of God in such a time. They said, in effect, that the social iniquities of a nation could only bring disaster. Weakened by lack of inward integrity, the nation would easily collapse before pressure from the outside. Indeed, these very foreign nations, terrible as they were in their militarism, were veritable agents of God to bring about the necessary punishment of his recalcitrant people. Thus it was that in the first instance, the message of the prophets was that of doom.

Just because it is God, however, who is shaping history in accordance with his righteous will, there is hope for the future beyond the doom that is so imminent. After God has cast down, he will raise up again. Just because he is using even the heathen nations within the framework of his purpose, he will not allow them to triumph perpetually. When the people repent and return unto Jehovah he will establish them forever.

It is obvious that this teaching of the prophets did at least two things for their people. It provided for them a measure of understanding of the historical tragedies through which they passed, and it gave them faith and hope to look to the future with expectation of ultimate salvation.

46. What Are the Apocrypha?

In speaking of the Greek translation of the Old Testament, it was stated that that version contained a number of additional books which were not in the Hebrew canon. When the official Latin version of the Old Testament was made, these books were retained as a part of it but were named Apocrypha, meaning Hidden Books, or Books of Hidden Wisdom. Thus far, these books remained scattered throughout the Old Testament and in some cases were incorporated as parts of already existing books. Martin Luther, however, grouped all the apocryphal writings together in a single section. Today, if they are included at all in our Bibles, as they well should be, they form a group of fourteen books located between the Old Testament and the New Testament.

For the most part these books were composed between 200 B.C. and A.D. 100. Thus, they overlap the end of the Old Testament and the beginning of the New Testament, and provide valuable sources for the period in between. In general, the religious character of these books is probably not quite as high as that of the books in the regular canon. Nevertheless, the Apocrypha contain many elevated and beautiful passages.

For a single example, we may cite a passage from the apocryphal book called Ecclesiasticus, or The Wisdom of Jesus the Son of Sirach. This is a long book of proverbs, written originally in Hebrew by a wise man of Jerusalem named Jesus ben Sirach, and some fifty years later translated into Greek by the author's grandson in Alexandria, Egypt. One section of the book tells about different kinds of laborers including the farmer, the craftsman, the builder, the painter, the smith, and the potter. Then this section concludes with the following very beautiful words which state that faithful doing of work is genuine prayer:

> All these rely on their hands;
> And each one is skilful in his own work;
> Without them, no city can be inhabited,
> And men will not live in one or go about in it.
> But they are not sought for to advise the people,
> And in the public assembly they do not excel.
> They do not sit on the judge's seat,
> And they do not think about the decision of lawsuits;
> And they do not utter instruction or judgment,
> And they are not found using proverbs.
> Yet they support the fabric of the world,
> And their prayer is in the practice of their trade.[1]

47. What Was the Purpose of Apocalyptic Literature?

Apocalyptic literature comprises an important part of the religious writings of the first few centuries B.C. and A.D. In the Old Testament, the book of Daniel and portions of Ezekiel, Joel, Isaiah, and Zechariah are of this type. In the Apocrypha, II Esdras is the outstanding example. Among the Pseudepigrapha, which is the designation Professor R. H. Charles gives to a further body of books, all composed under the names of famous characters of the past, there are apocalyptic books ascribed to Baruch, Enoch, Isaiah, Moses, Solomon, the twelve patriarchs, and the Sibyl. In the New Testament, there is one book of this kind. It is called the Apocalypse in the Greek, and is known to us by the English translation of that word as the Revelation.

---

[1] 38:31–34. *The Apocrypha, An American Translation*, by Edgar J. Goodspeed. Quoted by permission of the publishers, The University of Chicago Press.

The essential interest of the apocalyptic writings is denoted by that word "revelation." They desire to draw back the veil of the future and show, as Revelation 1:1 puts it, "the things which must shortly come to pass." The times in which these books were written were evil. The Jews were suffering oppression under the Syrians or the Romans; the Christians were being persecuted on account of emperor worship. For the most part, the apocalypses despair of human action to renovate the social order. They are not expressions of pessimistic resignation, however, but of invincible faith. They believe there is more to the universe than man and his wrong-doings. They believe in God, they believe that it is his eternal purpose to establish righteousness, and they believe that his intervention to this end is imminently to be expected. Therefore, they summon the true believers to steadfast endurance in anticipation of certain salvation.

It was characteristic of the apocalyptic writers to employ many visions and symbols. Particularly because it was a time of persecution, they used obscure illusions and cryptic hints. The most famous example of this is the number of the beast which is given in Revelation 13:18 as 666. It is almost certain that this was a cryptogram for the name of Caesar Nero, whose return as a demonic destroyer was expected. It is necessary, therefore, to study the apocalyptic writings in the settings of their own times, but it is also right to apply their invincible faith to the problems of our day.

48. How Was the Life of Christ Recorded?

There is only one place where Jesus is said to have written anything. This is in John 8:6, where it is stated that "Jesus bent down and wrote with his finger on the ground."

Whatever words he traced in the sand at that time must
have been soon obliterated by the passing breeze or the
trampling feet of men. Otherwise, as far as our information
goes, Jesus did not himself write down any records. Since
there is also no indication of any stenographer's writing
down his words as they were uttered, we must assume that
at first the sayings of Jesus and the memory of his actions
as well were simply preserved in the minds of his hearers
and those who associated with him. That there was such
a period of oral transmission is not surprising in the least;
and, as a matter of fact, it was, comparatively speaking,
very brief. In the case of the earlier Old Testament records,
some of the materials must have been handed down by
word of mouth for hundreds of years. In India, there are
important religious texts which were transmitted orally for
a thousand years.

The first written records concerning Christ were probably collections of his sayings. We do not have any ancient
examples, but we have a striking sample from the third
century A.D. This is a sheet of papyrus which was found
at the Egyptian town of Oxyrhynchus. The papyrus contains a series of sayings, each introduced with the words,
"Jesus saith." Some of the sayings are ones which are also
to be found in the canonical gospels; but others would
be totally unknown to us save for their fortunate preserva-
tion upon this long-buried fragment of papyrus. It seems
reasonable to suppose that other collections of the sayings
of Jesus had been made at early dates. As a matter of fact,
one such extended collection of sayings was, we now
think, the earliest written record about the life of Christ.
This collection was used as a major source in the compila-
tion of the first and third gospels, those bearing the names
of Matthew and of Luke. There is a strong possibility that
the collection of sayings was originally made by the apostle

Matthew, and that it is for this reason that his name is attached to the gospel in which these sayings were later incorporated. Since the collection was a very important source, German scholars often referred to it by their corresponding word, *Quelle*. From this, we derive the customary designation of this hypothetical source as "Q."

The next thing that happened after the composition of "Q," as far as we are able to trace the course of events, was the writing of the Gospel according to Mark. Early church tradition ascribes this work to Mark, the companion of Paul and Peter, and leads us to believe that it was written at Rome, shortly after Peter lost his life there in the Neronian persecution. This would seem to be a very natural situation. When the great apostle was gone and other eyewitnesses of the life of Jesus had also died or were growing old, it became very necessary to commit the record of the life of Christ to writing. On the whole, Mark's gospel may be characterized as a swift account of the things which Jesus did.

The next step was then, logically enough, the combining of the account of the doings of Christ with the collection of his sayings. This was essentially what was accomplished in the gospels according to Matthew and to Luke. The name of Matthew's gospel has already been given a tentative explanation. The third gospel is believed to have been written by Luke, who was "the beloved physician" and the companion of Paul. In the preface to this gospel, Luke tells how by that time many narratives of the life of Christ had been compiled and how he had traced all things closely and endeavored to write an orderly account of the life of Christ. In Matthew and Luke, the main sources are Mark and "Q," while many other materials have been gathered from yet other sources.

To these three written gospels, a fourth was later added,

the Gospel according to John. It is in the nature of a profound and penetrating meditation upon the innermost significance of the life of Christ. All of these gospels were written in the first century A.D., and in the second century, the writer, Irenaeus, was able to declare that even as there are four regions of the world and four principal winds, so too the Church, which is scattered over the whole earth, has four strong foundation pillars, namely the four gospels.

49. Why Did Paul Write Letters?

The letters of Paul were probably written before any of the four gospels, which we have just mentioned. Thus, Paul's letters are the earliest written parts of the New Testament which we now have. It is, therefore, very interesting to ask why it was that Paul came to write these letters.

As we remember, Paul journeyed widely across the Mediterranean world. He believed that Christianity was for everybody, not just for the Jewish people among whom Jesus had lived. The only requirement for a Christian, he taught, is faith, which is an attitude of loving trust in God, through Jesus Christ. Therefore, Paul went constantly to new places to tell new people this universal message. As he went, sometimes he wanted to write ahead to prepare for his coming, and more often, matters came up after he had left a place, which required his attention and called for a communication. In other words, he wrote his letters on all kinds of occasions, naturally connected with the carrying out of his work.

To make this general statement more specific, we may give a few concrete examples. Paul preached the gospel at Thessalonica and afterward sent his associate, Timothy, back to see how matters were, there. He himself, meanwhile, was at Athens and Corinth. When Timothy returned Paul wrote two letters to express his joy at the good news which Timothy brought and also to give advice on certain problems which Timothy reported had arisen in the church at Thessalonica. These problems included the death of some of the church members, and also the abandonment of work by others who believed that the end of the world would take place any moment.

Not long after this Paul received word of what had happened over in the Roman province of Galatia in Asia Minor. There he had preached his universal gospel of faith, but afterward certain "Judaizers" had come in and said that it was necessary for any pagan to become a Jew first before he could be a Christian. Paul immediately wrote a vehement letter to declare that Abraham himself had been characterized by faith and that, therefore, anyone who had faith was a spiritual descendant of his and an heir of the promises which God had made to him. Therefore, anyone could be a Christian directly by faith.

Later Paul wrote a series of letters to the church at Corinth where many problems had arisen, including sectarian divisions, pagan life, attacks on Paul himself, and perplexities about spiritual gifts and the resurrection. Again Paul wrote a lengthy letter to Rome to prepare for his own visit to the Christian church in that capital of the world.

Paul went to Rome at last, but, sadly enough, as a prisoner. Even so, he could continue writing letters and he did so to churches which had sent him help and which had problems of various kinds.

Paul wrote letters to individuals as well as to churches, and among these perhaps the most striking is a short one-page note to the master of a runaway slave. Paul had converted the runaway slave to Christianity and was sending him back to the master, himself a Christian. In this short

letter, he asked the master to receive the runaway back
again, "no longer as a slave but more than a slave, as a beloved brother."

Such were the kinds of situations in which Paul penned
his letters. All together he wrote more than a dozen which
were eventually gathered from the places to which he had
sent them and made into a collection and an important
part of our New Testament.

50. How Do We Know That We Are Reading What the Original Writers Wrote?

When we read the Bible, how do we know that we are
reading what the original writers of the documents wrote?
The answer to this question involves telling something
about the branch of study which is known as textual criticism. The work in this field of research includes the discovery of ancient manuscripts and the careful comparison
of all such manuscripts that are known anywhere, in order
to find which are the oldest manuscripts and what is the
true text, as far as it can be recovered, of the Bible.

Illustrating the story with particular reference to the
New Testament, we may begin by reporting that the oldest fragment of a New Testament manuscript now known
is a bit of papyrus containing a few words of the Gospel
according to John from a copy which was made in the
first half of the second century A.D. After that, the next
oldest important manuscript is a copy of the collection of
Paul's letters, also written on papyrus and dating from
around A.D. 200. Then from around A.D. 350, we have
the great parchment manuscripts, the Vaticanus, kept in
the Vatican library at Rome, and the Sinaiticus, now
in the British Museum at London. After that there is an
ever-increasing number of manuscripts as we come down

across the centuries. All together, there are over two thousand five hundred manuscripts which bear witness to the text of the New Testament.

The comparison of these manuscripts with each other is a very painstaking task. By this labor, it is possible to group the manuscripts into several great families and to determine at least approximately which are the oldest ones. The various manuscripts do not always exactly agree in their wording, both because scribes often made mistakes in copying and also because intentional changes were sometimes made. It is necessary, therefore, to study every word in the text and see how it reads in the various manuscripts, particularly in the oldest ones. Thus it is often possible to detect and correct mistakes and changes which have been made. Of course, every time a new manuscript is discovered, it has to be compared with the ones already known to see if it brings us any additional information. By this long process of scientific work, it is possible to establish the original text of the New Testament with, in most cases, a very high degree of accuracy.

It is because this work is constantly going on and because some of the oldest manuscripts have been discovered in recent years, that it has been necessary to make new translations of the Bible from time to time. The newest translations, based upon the most ancient manuscripts, are extremely accurate.

51. What Is the Best Translation of the Bible?

The preceding discussion has shown the necessity of making new translations of the Bible from time to time. In general, the translations which have been made may be grouped into two classes. The first class includes the translations made by large bodies of scholars who had some more or less official authorization to undertake the task. Of the English translations produced by such groups of scholars, the most famous is the Authorized, or "King James" Version which was published and dedicated to King James in A.D. 1611. Written in simple, stately, beautiful, and vigorous language, the words of this translation have entered deeply into common speech and general literature. In the judgment of such a distinguished representative of literary pursuits as Mary Ellen Chase, who has devoted one of her books to *The Bible and the Common Reader*, it is the King James Version which is best suited to the uses of the ordinary reader.

With the availability of new manuscripts in the nineteenth century, particularly including Codex Vaticanus which was only then made accessible to outside scholars, and Codex Sinaiticus which was only then discovered in its remote monastery, the necessity for a scholarly revision seemed evident. Such a Revised Version was published in England in 1881 and in America in 1901. Again, in the twentieth century a new revision is being produced. Using yet later discoveries and more accurate still, this is the Revised Standard Version, of which the New Testament appeared in 1946.

The second general category of translations comprises those made independently by individual scholars or small groups of scholars. Among the most notable of these are the *New Translation* by James Moffatt and the *American Translation* by J. M. Powis Smith, Edgar J. Goodspeed, and others. In general, such translations as these are not only very accurate, but also extremely modern in phraseology. Sometimes, too, they make rearrangements in the text in accordance with recent scholarly theories.

All of the translations mentioned and others, too, have their great values. Which is "best" to use depends to a considerable extent upon the particular purpose we have in mind at the time. All are valuable aids to our study of the Word of God.

52. What Is the Biblical View of Human Destiny?

The biblical view of human origins is found in the book of Genesis. Man was created by God as a being with a spiritual nature, capable of fellowship and co-operation with his Creator.

The biblical view of human history is found in the Prophets. Man, both individually and collectively, rebels against the purpose of God and thereby brings disaster upon himself and his society. In the light of the righteousness of God, and under the circumstances of man's sinfulness, this is an inevitable result. The prophets sometimes used the figure of a plumb line, to suggest that even as a wall that is found to be crooked cannot stand but will eventually collapse under the ceaseless pull of the force of gravity, so, too, a nation whose life is not right will fall. The nature of God is also that of love, however, and therefore the prophets declared with equal assurance that if only a man or nation would repent, a way of restoration would be opened.

The biblical view of human destiny suggested already in the hope of the prophets, is worked out in the New Testament. It is that there will be at last a kingdom of Heaven in which the will of God will be done perfectly. This kingdom is expected to come "on earth," yet since "the things which are seen are temporal" its final place must be in an eternal world which is now unseen.

Is it the ultimate destiny of all mankind to attain to this kingdom? The answer to this question no man can know. The book of Revelation pictures the symbolic number of 144,000 persons singing praises to God on the shore of the sea that is like glass mingled with fire, while torment and woe are poured out upon the ungodly. The 144,000 are the martyrs in the persecution of Domitian; the others are the worshipers of the Beast. Surely there must be a difference like that in the destinies of the good and the evil.

Nevertheless, the apostle Paul seems to look forward to an ultimate outcome of God's purposes in an all-comprehending redemption. He views all human history as symbolized in the two epochal figures of Adam and of Christ. The former he equates with sin and death, the latter with obedience and life. Then he declares, "For as in Adam all die, so also in Christ shall all be made alive" (I Corinthians 15:22). Again, in Romans 11:32, Paul declares, "God hath shut up all unto disobedience, that he might have mercy upon all." In *The Bible Today*, Professor C. H. Dodd interprets the last passage to mean that "as every human being lies under God's judgment, so every human being is ultimately destined, in his mercy, to eternal life." Similarly in Ephesians 1:10 and Colossians 1:20 it is declared to be God's purpose to "sum up all things" or "reconcile all things" in Christ. The last goal is "that God may be all in all" (I Corinthians 15:28). "This," says Professor Dodd, speaking of the Biblical view, "is the final meaning of the entire process in time." [1]

For Further Reading

Walter Russell Bowie, *The Bible*. New York, Association Press, 1940.

Mary Ellen Chase, *The Bible and the Common Reader*. New York, The Macmillan Company, 1944.

[1] *The Bible Today*. 1947, pp. 118f. Quoted by permission of the publishers, the Cambridge University Press.

C. H. Dodd, *The Bible Today*. Cambridge, Cambridge University Press, 1947.

Jack Finegan, *Light from the Ancient Past*. Princeton, Princeton University Press, 1946.

Harry Emerson Fosdick, *A Guide to Understanding the Bible*. New York, Harper and Brothers, 1938.

R. M. Grant, *The Bible in the Church*. New York, The Macmillan Company, 1948.

Edgar J. Goodspeed, *How to Read the Bible*. Philadelphia, The John C. Winston Company, 1946.

Alice Parmelee, *A Guidebook to the Bible*. New York, Harper and Brothers, 1948.

G. Ernest Wright, *The Challenge of Israel's Faith*. Chicago, The University of Chicago Press, 1944.

7

THE CHURCH

53. When Did the Church Originate?

THE WORD "church" is the English translation of the Greek word *ecclesia*, from which root we get such a word as "ecclesiastical." *Ecclesia* meant fundamentally an assembly, and in relation to Christianity denoted a gathering or a company of Christians. It could be used either for a single group of Christians in one locality or for the whole body of Christians everywhere.

Upon asking when the church originated, we come upon two somewhat surprising facts. The first is, that in the gospels the word church hardly ever appears. Its only occurrences are in Matthew 16:18 and 18:17. This is apparently conclusive proof that Jesus said little or nothing about any formal organization of his disciples. The second fact is that in the letters of Paul, the first of which were written within twenty years after the crucifixion of Christ, there is constant mention of the church and it is clearly an organization of much importance and vitality. Two conclusions may be drawn from the two facts just observed. The first conclusion is that during the lifetime of Jesus what later became the church was growing up only silently and naturally as an informal fellowship. The second, that whereas the death of the Leader might have been expected to destroy this incipient association, on the contrary something happened very soon thereafter to make it stronger than ever. According to the traditions of the church itself, what happened was the resurrection of Christ on the first

day of the week after his death and the special realization
of the influence of his spirit which came to the disciples
sometime after that on the day of Pentecost.

If the foregoing description of the historical circumstances is correct, then we would not expect to find that
Jesus had laid down any detailed blueprints for the organized life of his followers, nor would we expect that when
the church first came clearly into view it would be other
than a spontaneous growing thing. Actually this is exactly
the situation which is reflected in the documents of the
New Testament. In the gospels, we see the disciples eating,
journeying, working with Christ. In the letters of Paul,
particularly the earlier ones, we see the Christians with a
variety of officers and leaders, finding their way gradually
toward the most effective form of Christian community.
Only in the later writings are the outlines of organization
coalescing into quite definite forms. We would say, then,
as we look at the whole picture, that the church is not
artificial but natural, and that it came into being not as
something arbitrarily imposed upon men but as something
spontaneously growing up out of the tremendous impact
of the life of Christ in the history of the world.

54. What Is the Roman Catholic Church?

The Roman Catholic Church is the form which Christianity assumed as time went along, particularly insofar as
it was centered around Rome. Already in the first century
A.D., the growing Christian movement faced many problems. There was a tendency for the Christians to divide
into sects, as we saw in connection with Paul's correspondence with the Corinthians. There were also problems
of philosophy and of varying teachings on religious subjects, as we may clearly learn from such a letter as that

which Paul wrote to the Colossians. In the second century A.D. all of these problems continued to exist and even grow more acute. In order to help meet them, the Christian community developed three things which were scarcely on the horizon in the first century.

The first was the bringing together of the most important Christian writings that had by then been composed into a canon of officially recognized scripture. This canon was not defined with absolute finality for another century or two, but the main outlines of it emerged clearly in the second century. In its essential structure, it comprised the four gospels and the letters of Paul and other "apostles," these two main parts being connected by the book of Acts. Most of these documents were written originally, no doubt, without any anticipation that they would ever be embodied in such an official collection. Nevertheless, the grouping together of all of these documents and their acceptance as authoritative, provided materials of extreme importance for the guidance of the growing church.

The second development was the formulation of the Apostles' Creed, a short paragraph of condensed Christian belief, which could be used as a test and standard of what it really was to be a Christian. The central ideas of this creed are of course derived from the first century Christian writings, but those writings, themselves, had not contained such a creed in any formalized way.

The third thing was the acceptance of the authority of a single bishop in each city. In the twelfth chapter of I Corinthians, we read about a variety of workers in the church, including apostles, prophets, teachers, workers of miracles, healers, helpers, administrators, and speakers in various kinds of tongues. In the letters to Timothy and Titus we hear about bishops, elders, and deacons. The nature of the references is such that we can hardly tell whether the bishop and the elder are at this time one and the same functionary, or different. As the second century advanced, however, the bishop was more and more exalted and the authority of a single bishop in a single city was more and more recognized. To have the right to such authority, the bishop was supposed to have received his commission in a direct line of descent from the apostles.

The emergence of these three things, the New Testament Canon, the Apostles' Creed, and the Apostolic Episcopate (*Episcopos* being the Greek word for bishop), is generally recognized as marking the outlines of the developing Roman Catholic Church. But where does the Roman part come in? The answer lies in the fact that the city of Rome was then the capital of the world. Naturally, therefore, the bishop in that city tended to exert a corresponding authority over all Christians everywhere. This authority was heightened by the fact that the two great apostles, Peter and Paul, had both worked and died in Rome. Indeed, the church at Rome believed it possible to trace the commission of its head back through an unbroken succession to Peter himself. This head of the Roman church, who, by virtue of the city in which he presided and of the commission which he was said to have from Peter, claimed authority over all Christians everywhere, eventually became known as the Pope.

55. What Is the Eastern Orthodox Church?

The Roman ideal was a church that was "always and everywhere the same." Christians did not everywhere and always agree to the leadership of Rome, however. Other cities in addition to Rome had ancient Christian communities and honorable Christian leaders. Besides Rome, the other most important cities were doubtless Constantinople, Alexandria, Antioch, and Jerusalem. While Rome dominated the West, these other four cities tended to form a group in the East. As a matter of fact, each of these cities was the center of a patriarchate or extended ecclesiastical region under the jurisdiction of a bishop who was called a patriarch. From this point of view the patriarchates of Constantinople, Alexandria, Antioch, and Jerusalem formed the Eastern Church, as opposed to the Western Church which comprised the patriarchate of Rome.

The actual division between the East and the West was something that only came about gradually. Contributing forces were political rivalries, linguistic differences, the East speaking Greek and the West Latin, and temperamental differences, the East being interested in philosophy and the West being prevailingly practical. The consummation of a long drift apart came in the so-called Great Schism in A.D. 1054. At that time, the Roman Pope, Leo IX, and the patriarch of Constantinople, Michael Cerularius, came into controversy. On July 15, 1054, the legates of Leo placed a decree in the great church of Hagia Sophia which excommunicated Cerularius and all his adherents and called down upon him condemnation "along with all heretics, together with the devil and his angels." The division between East and West which was made irrevocable by that action has continued until today. By the Eastern Orthodox Church is meant not only the patriarchates already mentioned, but also other churches founded in the East, for example in the Balkans and in Russia, which likewise are not in communion with Rome.

56. What Is Protestantism?

Protestantism is a movement which arose in the West, and which resulted in a major breaking away from the

Roman Catholic Church. This movement was inaugurated by Martin Luther, himself a Roman Catholic monk in Germany. In the course of profound spiritual struggles, he devoted himself to the study of the New Testament, particularly Paul's letter to the Romans. Finding there the words, "the just shall live by faith," Luther was greatly helped. He began to see that a Christian can go directly to God by faith without the necessity for the mediation of an elaborate ecclesiastical organization. At the same time he became increasingly aware of various abuses within the ecclesiastical machine of which he was a part. The most glaring of these was the peddling of "indulgences." Although the theological definition of it was more refined, an indulgence appeared to the ordinary Christian to be a pardon for his sin and a remission of its penalties purchasable for a certain fee. When a vendor of such indulgences was coming to his city of Wittenberg, Luther challenged the practice in a series of ninety-five theses, which he posted on the door of the castle church and declared himself ready to defend. This event took place in A.D. 1517.

From then on, the controversy developed rapidly and a large number of people rallied to the support of the stand which was being taken by the young monk. Originally, Luther had no thought save that of the correction of certain abuses within the Roman Catholic Church. Ultimately he found himself the leader of a movement which broke away entirely and assumed its own proportions. Among the ideas characteristic of the new movement were those which grew naturally out of the very experience of Martin Luther. These included the reading of the Bible by every man for himself, and the acceptance of the doctrine of justification by faith, whereby every individual Christian had the dignity and the liberty of a direct relationship to God through Christ.

These ideas and others related to them proved immensely effective in the minds of men. They spread rapidly and soon there were other leaders in other lands, promulgating similar and related teachings. These leaders included Zwingli and Calvin in Switzerland, John Knox in Scotland, John Wesley in England, and many others in many other places. It was as a result of all these movements, dedicated to freedom and to faith, that Protestantism arose.

57. Why Are There So Many Different Churches?

In the foregoing, we have seen how the three major divisions of Christendom came into existence, namely Roman Catholicism, Eastern Orthodoxy, and Protestantism. While the Roman Catholic Church has substantially maintained its unity and exists as one centralized ecclesiastical organization, there are many separate churches within Eastern Orthodoxy and an almost endless number and variety of bodies within Protestantism. Why are there so many different churches? Let us take up this important problem where it is most acute, namely within Protestantism itself.

An essential principle of Protestantism is, as we have seen, that each man should read the Bible for himself and go for himself directly to God through faith in Christ. If each man may read, study, and interpret the Bible for himself there is nothing to keep him, as he does so, from thinking his own thoughts and arriving at his own conclusions. This is exactly what Protestants have done. Set free from the restraining influence of a centralized authority, and inspired by the joy of free perusal of God's word, each group has gone in its own direction.

This is obviously a great and good thing. It means that, unhampered by exterior compulsion, men are following the dictates of their own intellect and conscience in the things of religion. Such liberty is the very genius of Protestantism.

On the other hand, certain of the consequences of this attitude have been lamentable. According to the *Yearbook of American Churches* for 1945, there were at that time 256 religious bodies in the United States of America. The Roman Catholic Church was shown as one, the Jewish congregations were counted as one body, and it was the Protestants who accounted for almost all the rest of these numerous groups. Surely it is carrying the principle of Protestantism too far when it results in such an excessive fragmentation. Or perhaps the situation results from the over-emphasis upon one principle to the neglect of another. The principle of freedom is certainly implicit in Protestantism and precious to it. But there is another principle in Christianity which should also be cherished and practiced by Protestantism, namely the principle of fellowship. Fellowship is just as biblical as freedom. If we study the Bible and derive from it the great teaching of faith which enables each of us to stand up in freedom and dignity before God, we need also to pay heed to the other teaching which was also set forth by the apostle Paul when he appealed to the divided Corinthians, "that all of you agree and that there be no dissensions among you, but that you be united in the same mind and the same judgment."

58. What Are the Distinctive Emphases of Some of the Churches?

As each body of Christians has followed the leading of that portion of the light which has come to it out of God's word, it has developed certain distinctive emphases. Let us try to describe some of these.

When one enters a Roman Catholic Church, one is impressed by a sense of historical continuity. Napoleon assembled his men for the Battle of the Pyramids and told them, "Forty centuries of history look down on you." In a Roman Catholic Church, nearly twenty centuries of Christian history seem to look down on us. The language used is still that of antiquity, the prayers offered by the priests express the same thoughts which are represented in the paintings of the catacombs beneath Rome.

The Eastern Orthodox Church is distinguished by its mysticism. This may be vividly realized from the great church of Hagia Sophia at Constantinople. Here the very architecture is such as to give a sense of the brooding presence of the Spirit of God and of the ineffable beauty and peace of that presence.

The Lutheran Church is marked by faith, such as Martin Luther himself taught so strongly. In her book, *Until That Day*, Kressmann Taylor told how in the days of Hitler the members of a Lutheran congregation in Berlin assembled only to find their church roped off and entrance barred by Storm Troopers. They waited a long time, hoping to be able to worship. At last they began to move away. As they did so, someone started Martin Luther's hymn, *Ein' feste Burg*. All the voices took it up and they marched away, down the radiating streets, giving expression to an undefeatable faith in the words:

> A mighty fortress is our God,
> A bulwark never failing,
> Our helper he, amid the flood
> Of mortal ills prevailing.
>
> And though this world, with devils filled,
> Should threaten to undo us,
> We will not fear, for God hath willed
> His truth to triumph through us.

The Episcopal Church has placed a distinctive emphasis upon beauty. Concerning one of its great cathedrals, Dr. Ralph Adams Cram spoke as chief architect, "This building will stand for a minimum of 2,000 years and will minister to 20,000,000 people in that time. Suppose it does cost $30,000,000? A super-dreadnaught costs as much, serves a destructive end, and at the end of twenty-five years has to be scrapped." Such is the importance attached to the making of a beautiful place for the worship of God in the traditions of this church.

The Presbyterian Church has been marked by its devotion to the exposition of the Bible. Its ministers have excelled in expository preaching, and as they have explained a single word of sacred writ, it has become luminous and vitally effective. The Methodist Church has been characterized by the spirit of the Crusade. Charles and John Wesley preached and sang their warm-hearted message throughout England, and soon thereafter Robert Raikes began to gather children into Sunday Schools, John Howard took up the struggle for prison reform, and Wilberforce began his battle against slavery. The Congregational Church has stood for freedom, and it was from its circles that the Pilgrim Fathers came to America. The Baptist Church has staunchly advocated the separation of church and state, and has risen to the defense of this great principle at every crisis. The Disciples of Christ have pleaded for unity in the midst of a divided Christendom. The Society of Friends has explored the silences and derived strength and insight from waiting quietly for the light to shine within the human soul.

Such are some of the distinctive emphases of some of the churches. Certainly no single church has a monopoly on any single emphasis which we have mentioned. Yet each has made the one mentioned a specially characteristic mark of its common life. As we survey them all, these various emphases would seem to be not contradictory but complementary aspects of the total life of Christendom.

59. What Attitude Should I Take toward People of Other Beliefs?

As we look at the whole multifarious and variegated picture of the existing Christian world, we sometimes see aspects of it which strike us as strange. Some names seem queer and some practices peculiar. In such a situation, it is helpful to remember the words, "No great soul ever laughed at anything that was sacred to another soul." Instead of reacting with scorn toward that which is unfamiliar to ourselves, it seems desirable to strive for sympathetic understanding. As a matter of fact, what we ourselves believe may appear queer to someone else! Therefore, it behooves us all to be considerate of one another's beliefs.

This does not, of course, mean that one will never make any choices as to what he himself wishes to believe. The total variety of belief and practice is so great that one person can hardly comprehend it all in his own mind and behavior. He is necessarily driven to select that formulation of faith and that method of expression which seem to him most nearly in accord with the truth and in harmony with his own needs and aspirations. Thus, it may well be that there will continue to be varieties of faith and practice in line with varying understanding and need; but among all these religious groups let us have the grace of mutual appreciation.

60. Cannot One Be as Good a Christian
without Joining the Church?

Whitehead's famous definition of religion as "what the individual does with his own solitariness," suggests that much of religion is a highly personal matter. It relates to the inmost self of a person in his deepest thoughts, highest aspirations, and most solitary communion with God. Certainly an important part of Christianity is to pray and to read the Bible for ourselves, and for each in his own place and way to do good to those about him. This should be done with so little public display that even the right hand does not know what the left does.

Jesus spoke kindly of ones who served the kingdom of God even in isolation from the group of disciples. Some of the disciples protested to him about a man they had seen casting out demons in the name of Christ. "We forbade him," they said, "because he was not following us." But Jesus rebuked that attitude on the part of his own disciples and declared, "He that is not against us is for us."

On another occasion, however, Jesus said plainly, "He who is not with me is against me, and he who does not gather with me scatters." This gives necessary emphasis to the other side of the matter. Certainly being a solitary Christian is important, but being a social Christian is even more important. As we have already pointed out, the very essence of Christianity includes the conceptions of Agape, or concern for others, and fellowship, or togetherness in the spirit of Christian love. Furthermore, the solitary Christian neglects the law of the necessity of co-operation for the accomplishment of major tasks. It is by no accident that Jesus made some of his most precious promises to his disciples conditional upon their togetherness: "Again I say to you, if two of you agree on earth about anything they ask, it will be done for them by my Father in heaven. For where two or three are gathered in my name, there am I in the midst of them."

The story is told of a group of tribal chieftains sitting in council. Each had his own plan for meeting a threatened attack. An old and wise chief then gave each man a single stick and told him to break it. Each did so without difficulty. Gathering the same number of sticks again, the old chief bound them together into a bundle. This he passed to each man, bidding him try to break it. Not even the strongest was now able to do so. Thus, the wise chieftain enforced the necessity of their unity. That is why one cannot be as good a Christian without joining the church. In the church he bands himself together with others for common prayer and common work. Answers can come to prayers that are made by people together and success can attend work that is done by people together which could not be otherwise.

61. Should One Be Baptized?

There are a few very high-minded people, notably including the Quakers, who feel that religion is so completely a spiritual matter that no outward thing is essential to it. Perhaps that is true, but it is also true that for most people the existence of at least some outward forms seems necessary and helpful.

If we turn directly to the New Testament, we are struck first by the action of Jesus himself. Free as he was in his disregard of the onerous restrictions which made the Sabbath a burden rather than a blessing to man, we might have expected that he would have had nothing to do with any ceremonies of any kind. Nevertheless, our oldest source, the Gospel according to Mark, introduces the public work of Jesus with the statement, "In those days Jesus came from Nazareth of Galilee and was baptized by John in the Jordan." John, as we know, was a remarkable man, a new prophet after there had been no prophet for a long time, who appeared in the wilderness, declared that the kingdom of God was near, and dipped beneath the waters of the Jordan River all who wished to prepare for it. And so it was that Jesus himself, too, came and was baptized. The symbolic act of baptism was not otherwise unknown at the time. We are aware, for example, that it was one of the things required of a proselyte to the Jewish faith. In the preaching of John and in the act of Jesus, however, baptism was clearly related to the kingdom of God.

Evidently those who became followers of Jesus also were baptized. For this, we have the statement of John 3:22: "After this Jesus and his disciples went into the land of Judea; there he remained with them and baptized." A parenthetical note in John 4:2 explains that Jesus himself did not baptize, but only his disciples. It was apparently somewhat in the same way as Jesus, that the apostle Paul also refrained for the most part from performing the actual act of baptism himself. The ceremony is described by Paul, however, as having the profoundest significance: "We were buried therefore with him by baptism into death, so that as Christ was raised from the dead by the glory of the Father, we too might walk in newness of life."

The answer to our question then would seem to be that one who wishes to be a Christian should be baptized. This is the outward tangible, symbolic act which signifies and manifests dedication to the kingdom of God. It has been hallowed by the example of Christ, illuminated by the interpretation of Paul, and honored by the acceptance of countless multitudes of persons across the centuries.

62. What Is the Significance of the Lord's Supper?

The Lord's Supper is the other ceremony along with baptism which has been observed in almost all the Christian churches throughout the centuries. We know from the gospels and from the eleventh chapter of I Corinthians that on the night before he was betrayed, Jesus ate a "last supper" with his disciples. This was a meal of fellowship held in an upper room somewhere in Jerusalem. Since the fact of his imminent death was clear to Jesus, although perhaps not to his disciples, and certainly not comprehended by them in its deepest significance, he performed a symbolic act to manifest it to them. In the words of the oldest account, as written by Paul, Jesus "took bread, and when he had given thanks, he broke it, and said, 'This is my body which is broken for you.' In the same way also the cup, after supper, saying, 'This cup is the new covenant in my blood.' " Essentially the same record stands in the synoptic gospels. In addition to the words we have already quoted, Paul states that in connection with the giving of the bread and the cup, Jesus said to his disciples, "Do this in remembrance of me." Since those words are not in the synoptic gospels, we cannot be absolutely sure of them. We can be certain, however, that the disciples at least from the time of Paul and probably from the very beginning, understood that they were to continue the breaking of the bread and the drinking of the cup as an act in memory of the Lord.

Several aspects of the significance of the Lord's Supper may therefore be indicated. First, it is a symbolic repetition of the last meal which Jesus ate on earth with his followers. Second, it is a setting forth in symbolic act instituted by himself, of the fact and significance of his death. In these two aspects, the emphasis is upon memory and the service may properly be called a memorial. In the third place, at the table of the Lord's Supper, there is a fellowship among the disciples and with the Lord. From this point of view, the service is rightly called communion, a word which is used in this connection already in I Corinthians 10:16. A fourth aspect of the service is that of anticipation and hope. According to Mark 14:25, Jesus said at the Last Supper, "I shall not drink again of the fruit of the vine until that day when I drink it new in the kingdom of God." And Paul said to the Corinthian Christians, "As often as you eat this bread and drink the cup, you proclaim the Lord's death until he comes." The Lord's Supper not only looks back to the death of Christ, but it also looks ahead to his ultimate triumph in the con- summation of all things. A fifth aspect of the service is suggested by the term Eucharist. This is derived from the Greek word for giving thanks, where it is said that Jesus gave thanks before he broke the bread to his disciples. In this light, the Lord's Supper is an expression of gratitude and thanksgiving to God. A sixth idea is connected with the service by the Roman Catholic Church, but not by the Protestant churches. This is that when the words of institution are uttered by the priest, the bread and wine are transformed into the body and blood of Christ and his sacrifice is repeated anew upon the altar.

63. Will the Churches Ever Unite?

One of the most encouraging signs in the whole Chris- tian movement today is the strong tendency toward unity. This manifests itself in the first place in a strong sense of sorrow for the many divisions of Christianity. A classic expression of this feeling was given in the following words at a modern world conference of churches: "We humbly acknowledge that our divisions are contrary to the will of Christ and we pray God in his mercy to shorten the days of our separation and to guide us by his spirit into fullness of unity."

A second mark of this tendency is a renewed emphasis upon the things in which the churches are already united. It is easy enough to put the emphasis upon the things by which we are separated. Instead of looking for these things, arguing about them, and magnifying them, there is a strong interest now in discovering, holding up, and making important the things on which all Christians already are agreed. There are surprisingly many of these things, and a genuine spiritual unity already exists among a great host of Christians who are superficially divided into separate bodies. Indeed, if it were not for the existence and steady growth of this underlying spiritual unity, it would be futile to talk about or strive for outward organizational unity.

A third mark of what is happening is the strengthening of co-operative movements among the churches. There are many kinds of these oriented towards various specific purposes. Some of these movements simply call themselves "Christian," without reference to denominationalism, and proceed with urgent tasks which lie before them. Thus, for example, we have the Young Men's Christian Association and the Young Women's Christian Association devoted to work with young men and women in the inclusive spirit of Christianity. Again we have organizations which make explicit recognition of the major divisions among religious bodies, all having their common background in the Bible, and endeavor to promote tolerance by the building of mutual understanding. Here one thinks, for example, of the National Conference of Christians and Jews, also known as the American Brotherhood.

Again there are councils of churches, organized on a community, state, national, or world basis. The bodies which are united in these organizations retain their autonomy, but co-operate voluntarily in common tasks. Speaking nationally, we have the Federal Council of the Churches of Christ in America; and looking to the world, we now have the World Council of Churches.

There is yet another level at which the achievement of Christian unity is progressing. This is the level of nothing less than organic union. Already some notable mergers of what were formerly separate denominations have taken place. In the United States they have been thus far for the most part within family groups of churches which already manifested great similarities. In South India, however, a scheme of union has been put into effect through which denominations with widely variant patterns of thought and organization have actually become one church.

Hitherto, to be entirely honest, we perhaps should have sung *Onward, Christian Soldiers* with the following words:

> Like a halting caravan
>   Moves the Church of Christ;
> We are feebly faltering
>   Toward our timid tryst.
> We are all divided,
>   Many bodies we,
> Kept apart by doctrine
>   And lack of charity.[1]

As a result of the many movements now in progress, some of which we have just described, the original words

---

[1] William H. Hudnut, Jr., in *The Christian Century*, April 26, 1944. Quoted by permission of the Editors.

of the hymn are becoming more and more truly applicable:

> Like a mighty army
>   Moves the Church of God;
> Brothers we are treading
>   Where the saints have trod;
> We are not divided,
>   All one body we,
> One in hope and doctrine,
>   One in charity.

For Further Reading

Kenneth S. Latourette, *Anno Domini*. New York, Harper and Brothers, 1940.

James H. Nichols, *Primer for Protestants*. New York, Association Press, 1947.

George Stewart, *The Church*. New York, Association Press, 1938.

Kressmann Taylor, *Until That Day*. New York, Duell, Sloan and Pearce, 1942.

Henry P. Van Dusen, *World Christianity, Yesterday, Today, Tomorrow*. Nashville, Abingdon-Cokesbury Press, 1947.

THE OTHER RELIGIONS

64. How Widespread Is Religion?

THUS FAR, we have spoken for the most part of our own religion, the basic documents of which are to be found in the Bible. Since the first part of the Bible is also the Scripture of Judaism, and since Jesus Christ, the founder of Christianity, was himself a member of the Jewish people, we have spoken often of matters which concern the Jewish faith as well as the Christian. Out beyond the Judeo-Christian tradition, however, there lie many other religions. Actually, religion is as widespread as the world. Everywhere, almost, where there are people, faith and religious practices are to be found.

There is an interesting illustration of this on the inside cover of Lewis Browne's *This Believing World*. There the author has drawn a sketch map, showing the religions which are dominant in various parts of the earth. All of the major continents are shown and some of the islands of the sea. Across each area is written the name of the faith which prevails there. Thus we find Moslems in Arabia, Hindus in India, Animists in Sumatra and Borneo, while the religions of Confucianism, Taoism, and Buddhism flourish in China, and that of Shinto in Japan. After having glanced over all these and the other areas, each properly labeled with its prevailing faith, we look at Greenland. There across the northern icy wastes is written the legend, "There is no religion in this region because there are no inhabitants." That is how it is in "this believing world."

Only where there are no people is there no religion.

Precise statistics on the various religions are difficult or impossible to obtain. It is hard enough to get a reasonably accurate census of religious bodies in the United States of America. In many other lands, little or no such attempt at a census has been made. Furthermore, in such a country as China the faith of any given individual may be compounded of elements from several different religions. Subject to such limitations, the following table gives an approximate statistical picture of the religions of the world.

Buddhism	155,000,000
Christianity	675,000,000
Confucianism	250,000,000
Hinduism	245,000,000
Islam	250,000,000
Jainism	1,000,000
Judaism	15,000,000
Primitive Religion	175,000,000
Shinto	20,000,000
Sikhism	5,000,000
Taoism	40,000,000
Zoroastrianism	100,000
Miscellaneous and no religion	168,900,000
Total World Population	2,000,000,000

65. When and How Did Religion First Begin?

Religion began as soon as man began. The emergence of humanity on earth and the emergence of religion came together. We have already noted that it is Neanderthal Man of 100,000 years ago who is the first representative of the modern genus or race of man. Neanderthal Man buried his dead. Instead of allowing the body of a deceased member of his family to lie like that of a beast, he interred it with some care and with some provision for the needs and welfare of that person in an after-life. Neanderthal Man had at least the beginnings of religious ideas. As we have also observed, Cro-Magnon Man of 50,000 years ago is regarded as the beginning of the species that today inhabits the earth. Cro-Magnon Man not only buried the dead but also practiced a notable art in the adornment of the walls of his caves with paintings. In these paintings there are unmistakably religious conceptions. The answer to the first part of our question is therefore clear. Religion began, as far as present evidence shows, 50,000 or 100,000 years ago along with the very beginning of human life itself.

How religion began is a question that is more difficult to answer. Some think that fear was the inspiring force, but others believe that from the very first reverence was mingled with apprehension. Some believe that the experience of dreams gave man the idea of the soul, and others think that man just naturally projected the sense of aliveness within himself into the objects of nature round him. Most investigators think that the idea of a spiritual force diffused through things and the idea of spirits animating individual objects were the earliest forms of religious belief. But some think that man began with a conception of one high God and afterward fell into superstition and polytheism.

In a comprehensive consideration of the rise of religion, we must at least note the three elements to which Harris Franklin Rall has called attention in his book on *Christianity*. Religion arises in the first place, Professor Rall there points out, from man's sense of need and from his search for life. In the second place, man has an awareness of an unseen world, a world of a higher order, upon whose ultimate forces his life is dependent. If the needs of man constitute the "push" of religion, the reality of this spiritual world is responsible for the "pull" of faith. The third aspect is that in which religion is at last actually present. It is when there is an active and reciprocal relation actually established between man and this higher world.

66. Who Are the Great Prophets of the Other Religions?

We have already noticed something of the importance of Moses for Judaism and of Jesus Christ in Christianity. In looking now at the other religions, we find that a number of these also have had great prophets. While some of these faiths grew from an almost immemorial antiquity through the thought and work of many unknown or little known persons, others definitely owe their rise to the appearance of great individual prophetic personalities. We will refer here to four such prophets.

Three of these lived roughly in the sixth century B.C., and one was born in the sixth century A.D. The first is Zoroaster, whose dates are traditionally given as 660–583 B.C. It may be that those dates should be a little later or possibly even as early as 1000 B.C. At all events, he was a man who grew up on the high plateau of Iran where there was a ceaseless struggle between the constructive forces of agriculture, herdsmanship, and civilization and the destructive forces of storms, wild animals, and barbarian inroads. In this setting, Zoroaster perceived a ceaseless universal struggle between good and light, and evil and darkness. He called upon men to join in the battle for the triumph of good and of light.

Gautama, who became the Buddha, lived in India around 560–480 B.C. He was of princely family and grew up amidst luxurious surroundings. Although it is said that his father tried to shield him from such sights, he eventually became aware of the existence of sickness, decrepitude, and death in the world. This awareness drove him to seek a profounder understanding of suffering and to find a way to escape from it. He left his home and family and went out into the jungle, searching. Going to the opposite extreme from his former mode of life, he adopted the most rigorous asceticism and almost starved himself to death. Finally deciding that that too, was not how to gain salvation, he adopted a middle way of right thought, conduct, and livelihood which he believed would lead at last to Nirvana, the blessed place where all desire, all striving, and all suffering are at an end.

Confucius lived in China about 551–478 B.C. He was a true sage who spent much of his time in the study of the literature of the ancient past. He believed that by studying what the wise men of yore had said, he could learn to arrange his own life and also organize society itself in harmonious patterns. For a time he held a high position in a small state in China and actually was very successful in carrying on a model government. He believed that if every man would begin by making his own thoughts right, it would work out finally so that his family, community, and nation also would enjoy right relationships. The fundamental principle of human relationship, he taught, was that of reciprocity.

Coming to a time about as long after the birth of Christ as these three men lived before it, we find Mohammed. He lived in Arabia, and the dates of his life were A.D. 570–632. He said that he received various visions and as a result of these he began to preach his religious doctrines. The main emphasis in his preaching was that there is only one God, whom he called Allah. This sounded strange to most of the Arabians, among whom, for the most part, polytheism had hitherto prevailed. Mohammed was not, therefore, at first successful with his teachings. Eventually, however, he left Mecca where he had been and went to Medina. There he found more people who were willing to listen to what he said, and at last he attained a great following and great power. Indeed, before he died he had united almost all of Arabia in his teachings and under his leadership. To this day the creed of his followers is, "There is no God but Allah and Mohammed is the Prophet of Allah."

67. Do the Other Religions Have Bibles Too?

Yes, all the living religions except those of primitive peoples do have characteristic collections of writings in which their doctrines are contained. The attitude toward these writings may vary from that in Confucianism where the classics are simply ancient texts embodying much wisdom, to that in Islam where the Koran is believed to have existed originally with Allah and to have been delivered piecemeal by the archangel Gabriel to the prophet Mohammed. A very brief indication of the nature of some of these "bibles" may now be given.

The sacred writings of Zoroastrianism are known as the Avesta, and particularly the part called the Gathas contains the sayings of the prophet Zoroaster. Here is one saying from that source. It is in the form of a prayer and contains the name of the Zoroastrian god of light, Ahura Mazda: "I who would serve you, O Mazda Ahura and Good Thought—do ye give through the Right the blessings of both worlds, the bodily and that of thought which set the faithful in felicity."

The sacred writings of Hinduism are very numerous. The

oldest are the Vedas, and the best known of all is doubtless the Bhagavad-Gita or "Song of God." Here are some words from the Gita: "Whose heart in pain is undismayed, who longeth not for pleasure, from whom desire, wrath, and fear have dropped, is called a sage of steady mind. Wherefore unattached perform those acts which are to be performed. Do thine allotted task, for work is better than inaction. For the man acting thus attaineth to the Supreme."

The Buddhist writings are also very extensive. The chief of these are found in three collections known as the Tripitaka or "Three Baskets." Here we may read of the preaching of the Buddha as follows: "There are two extremes from which he who leads the religious life must abstain. One is a life of pleasure, the other is a life of asceticism. The middle path is the noble Eight-fold Path: right belief; right resolve; right speech; right conduct; right occupation; right effort; right mindfulness; right contemplation. This is the middle path which opens the eyes and leads to peace of mind, to higher wisdom, to full enlightenment, to Nirvana."

The most highly regarded writings of Confucianism are the Five Classics and the Four Books. Among these we find the Analects, or sayings of Confucius. Here is one example from this source of the teaching of this great sage: "The Master said, In the presence of a good man, think all the time how you may learn to equal him. In the presence of a bad man, turn your gaze within!"

From the Koran, the sacred book of Islam, we quote this definition of religion: "Righteousness is not that ye turn your faces toward the east or toward the west, but righteousness is to believe in God, and the Last Day, and the angels and the Book, and the prophets; and to give of your wealth for love of God to kindred, to orphans, to the

needy and to the son of the road, to beggars and those
in captivity; and to be steadfast in prayer; and to be faithful
to your covenant when ye have made a covenant; and
patient in poverty and distress and in time of violence;
these are they who are true, and these are they who fear
the Lord!"

68. What Are Some of the Distinctive Emphases of Some of the Religions?

It is, of course, just as dangerous and difficult to try to
state in a few words the distinctive emphases of various
religions as it was to try to do the same thing for the
various denominations of Christianity. Any religion is itself a rich and varied thing which can hardly be compressed
into any single small formula. Especially Hinduism, for
example, has so many sides that any single thing which
is said about it is certainly both true and false at the same
time. Nevertheless, it should be possible to state at least
some one idea or emphasis which is particularly striking
in a great religion. We will try to do that for several of the
living faiths.

Zoroastrianism, which is a faith cherished today chiefly
by the Parsees of India, is notable for its strenuous ethical
concepts. It conceives the universe as the battleground of
two opposing forces, namely darkness and light. It calls
upon every man to choose his side and join in the conflict.
It believes that at last the god of light, Ahura Mazda,
together with his angels and all men who serve him, will
be victorious over the evil spirit, Angra Mainyu, and all
the hosts of darkness.

Hinduism is often characterized by pantheism. It believes that Brahman, the Soul of the Universe, is diffused
through all things like salt dissolved in water. It teaches

that when Atman, the soul of man, realizes its essential identity with Brahman it has attained salvation.

Buddhism teaches renunciation. It analyzes human suffering as arising fundamentally from man's desires. It reasons logically that the way to eliminate suffering is therefore to eradicate desire. He who achieves this completely will then be free from the painful cycle of transmigration and will enter into the passionless peace of Nirvana.

Confucianism inculcates filial piety. It wishes to organize all society in right relations and it views the relationship between father and son as the highest of all. Therefore, Confucianism contributes toward stability and conservatism in society.

A keynote of Islam is submission. Indeed, that is what the very name of the religion means and an individual adherent of it is called a Moslem or "One who has submitted." The submission is, of course, to the all-powerful will of the one God, Allah. There is, thus, in this religion a strong sense of the reality, majesty, and might of God. But there is also a definite tendency toward the fatalistic acceptance of whatever is.

69. What Do the Different Religions Believe about God?

This question has been partly answered in what we have said already, because we have given some of the names by which God is worshiped in some of the religions. Thus we are already familiar with the name of Ahura Mazda as the god of light and good in Zoroastrianism. Now we may explain that the word Ahura means "the Lord," and the word Mazda signifies "the all-knowing One." In order to bring out something more of the character of this deity here, we must also mention the Amesha Spentas or "undying holy ones." These are sometimes regarded as independent archangels, but there is also at least some justification for thinking of them as personified qualities of the one God. Therefore, when we find that their names are Good Thought, Right Order, Dominion, Piety, Health, and Immortality, we are given a clue as to the nature of Ahura Mazda.

Brahman, the Soul of the Universe in Hinduism, is difficult to describe as possessing any tangible attributes. The tendency in Hinduism is to feel that the ascription of any concrete characteristic to Brahman would imply a limitation. To say that Brahman is masculine or feminine, wise or good, would be to apply terms which come out of human experience and would therefore be inapplicable to the divine being. Therefore, Hinduism tends constantly to say "not that," "not that," when any defining term is applied to Brahman. The result is that the ultimate reality appears as a neuter, impersonal Absolute.

In both Buddhism and Confucianism, the original founders had relatively little to say about the gods. To Gautama Buddha, the numerous deities of polytheistic India were a part of the transitory, illusory world beyond which lay the Nirvana which he sought. To Confucius, it seemed desirable to maintain an attitude of aloof respectfulness toward the gods but to concentrate one's attentions upon the practical matters of human relationships. In the development which took place across the centuries, both Buddha and Confucius came to be regarded as deities by their followers, but such an idea was obviously far from the minds of these two prophets. The question has sometimes been raised, therefore, whether Buddhism and Confucianism should even be called religions. It seems proper to do so, however, because Buddhism bows before a supreme and inviolable order of things, and Confucianism speaks of the way of Heaven.

As for Allah, the one God of Islam, his chief attribute

is undoubtedly power. But to him the Koran ascribes no less than ninety-nine names in all, and these include such titles as: the Merciful, the Compassionate, the King, the Most Holy, the Tranquil, the Faithful, the Pardoner, the Rewarder, the Kind, the Answerer, the Friend, the Guide, the Lord of Glory and Honor.

70. Is There Anything on Which All the Religions Agree?

All the religions agree in belief in God. This fact we have set forth in answer to the preceding question, with due reference to the difficulty which arises in this connection in Buddhism and in Confucianism. We have maintained that all the religions, even including these two, believe in the existence of a supreme reality which is far above man and upon which man is dependent. The names which the religions apply to God are different and the attributes which they ascribe to him are varied. Nevertheless, the religions all stand together over against secularism and humanism in belief in that greater reality which men commonly call God.

All the chief living religions agree likewise in a second matter, namely, the essential principle which should control human relationships. This principle is that of reciprocity or the Golden Rule. It appears in no less than ten living religions in the following formulations:

BUDDHISM. Hurt not others with that which pains yourself.
CONFUCIANISM. Is there any one maxim which ought to be acted upon throughout one's whole life? Surely the maxim of loving-kindness is such—Do not unto others what you would not they should do unto you.
HINDUISM. This is the sum of duty: do naught to others which if done to thee, would cause thee pain.

ISLAM. No one of you is a believer until he loves for his brother what he loves for himself.

JAINISM. In happiness and suffering, in joy and grief, we should regard all creatures as we regard our own self, and should therefore refrain from inflicting upon others such injury as would appear undesirable to us if inflicted upon ourselves.

JUDAISM. What is hurtful to yourself do not to your fellow man. That is the whole of the Torah and the remainder is but commentary. Go learn it.

SIKHISM. As thou deemest thyself so deem others. Then shalt thou become a partner in heaven.

TAOISM. Regard your neighbor's gain as your own gain: and regard your neighbor's loss as your own loss.

ZOROASTRIANISM. That nature only is good when it shall not do unto another whatever is not good for its own self.

CHRISTIANITY. All things whatsoever ye would that men should do to you, do ye even so to them: for this is the law and the prophets.

It seems as if these two fundamental agreements of belief in God and of belief in the principle of the Golden Rule should provide a broad basis for unity and co-operation among all the religions. Certainly if we are to achieve the world unity which is now so desperately needed, we should have the united leadership of all religious forces.

71. How Can the Different Religions Be Evaluated?

Even though we recognize the fundamental agreements among religions which have just been indicated, we know that no single individual can believe in all the religions in the world. He must choose among them the faith which seems to him to embody the highest measure of truth and then draw from the others all the additional insights and help that he can. What criterion may be applied in the attempt to evaluate the various religions?

One criterion, which has been employed by Albert Schweitzer, is the distinction between world-negation and world-affirmation. Does the religion deny the world and try to escape from it, or does it accept the world and try to make something good in it and of it? Dr. Schweitzer himself maintains that the highest form of religion and the ideal of Christianity is "to live with the eyes fixed upon eternity, while standing firmly upon the solid ground of reality."

A second and somewhat related criterion is to ask whether a religion is pessimistic or optimistic. If it is pessimistic, it leads us to regard life as hopeless and man as helpless; if it is optimistic, it has some conception of a great purpose running through things, in the light of which even the most apparently insignificant life attains significance and the most apparently trivial task attains dignity.

A third test to apply is to ask whether a religion is less or more ethical. Some religions, by a negative conception of deity, make ethical conceptions seem relatively unimportant; others, by defining God himself in terms of righteousness and love, are thereby constrained to regard ethical conceptions as of the highest importance and ethical tasks as of the utmost urgency.

Such are some of the tests by which we can distinguish among the religions.

72. Should We Send Christian Missions to Lands Where Other Religions Exist?

Some people who become familiar with the facts we have set forth in the preceding sections draw the conclusion that Christian missions are irrelevant and indeed impertinent. Since there are already religions in all the lands, why trouble to send Christianity there, too? If a man has some kind of faith already, it is doubtless good enough for him and it is better to let the matter drop right there.

In thinking about this question, let us make a comparison with the realm of medicine. In all countries, there is at least some kind of practice of medicine. Even primitive men have their witch doctors who treat diseases with various herbs and spells. The attempt to heal is being carried on throughout the earth in one way or another. Therefore, if we were to argue along the lines set forth in the preceding paragraph, why should we be concerned to spread the practice of scientific medicine elsewhere in the world? The answer to that is, of course, obvious. There is a tremendous difference between the superstitious incantation of a primitive shaman and the skilled methods of a modern trained physician or surgeon. There is a difference between a concoction of herbs put together by trial and error and a scientifically compounded drug emanating from a modern laboratory. In other words, there are degrees in the apprehension of medical truth. A witch doctor is not to be despised if he is doing the best he can to relieve suffering according to the knowledge that he has, but he and his unfortunate patients should not be left in their relative darkness if we have something which would notably ameliorate their lot. They are human beings like ourselves and their fundamental physical needs are the same as our own.

Now coming back to the realm of spiritual things, shall we not likewise say that the fundamental need of man for God and for a way of life is essentially the same all around the world. The truth which can satisfy that need and sustain and nourish spiritual life must be fundamentally one and the same truth in all the world. Each religion has risen to attain its own portion of that truth, but all religions are not necessarily already on the same level of adequacy to meet basic human needs. The very best that is available anywhere should be shared as widely as possible and made accessible to all. Therefore, if Christianity, as we believe, represents the highest level of spiritual truth, we can no more properly keep it for ourselves than we can rightly retain for ourselves alone some advanced knowledge in the realm of medicine. As we carry Christianity to other lands then, we do not do so at all in the spirit of religious imperialism, to impose upon unwilling people something which we think they ought to have. Nor do we go to destroy what they have already attained. Jesus himself said about the religion which preceded him, "I came not to destroy, but to fulfil." The basic impulse in Christian missions is neither imperialistic nor destructive. It is the impulse of sharing. The idea of sharing is by no means incompatible with that of recognizing honestly, humbly, and gratefully all of the values which already exist in another faith. Indeed, it is to be hoped and believed that as we share Christianity with the adherents of another religion, Christianity itself will in turn be enriched and elevated. Insofar as Christianity is the truth, it has no need to fear these contacts; inasmuch as we believe it indeed to be the truth, we have the most urgent reason for carrying it everywhere.

For Further Reading

Vergilius Ferm, ed., *Religion in the Twentieth Century*. New York, Philosophical Library, 1948.

Florence M. Fitch, *Their Search for God*. Boston, Lothrop, Lee and Shepard Company, Inc., 1947.

Emma Hawkridge, *The Wisdom Tree*. Boston, Houghton Mifflin Company, 1945.

William E. Hocking, *Living Religions and a World Faith*. London, G. Allen and Unwin, Ltd., 1940.

Edward J. Jurji, ed., *The Great Religions of the Modern World*. Princeton, Princeton University Press, 1946.

Charles A. Moore, ed., *Philosophy—East and West*. Princeton, Princeton University Press, 1946.

F. S. C. Northrop, *The Meeting of East and West*. New York, The Macmillan Company, 1946.

Harris F. Rall, *Christianity*. New York, Charles Scribner's Sons, 1941.

PHILOSOPHIES OF RELIGION

73. What Is the Purpose of Philosophy of Religion?

PHILOSOPHY, as we have already explained, means the love of wisdom and thus signifies the quest for understanding. The philosophy of religion is then the quest for wisdom in the whole realm of religion. To put the matter into our own words, we might say that after we have gathered all the facts we can about the experiences, beliefs, and practices of all the denominations and all the historic and living religions, philosophy of religion is to look at the whole and ask, what is the essential truth in all of this?

It is customary to distinguish among three main areas of inquiry about religion, philosophy of religion being one of them. The first kind of study is known as the history of religion. As its name indicates, this involves exploring as far as possible the origins of religion and then tracing its development down across the centuries. Particular attention is necessarily paid to the great streams of tradition which constitute the religious developments in various lands. The founders of the faith are studied and their teachings, as well as the changes which were introduced by their followers across the years. The second type of inquiry is known as psychology of religion. Here investigation is directed toward the inward experiences, the mental, emotional, and spiritual states which are connected with religious belief and practice. Thus, the psychic states connected with the visions of Ezekiel or the revelations of Mohammed, the experiences involved in conversion and mysticism, and other such topics fall within the purview of psychology of religion.

After all the available data are in about the beliefs which man has cherished and about the effect of these beliefs in his own consciousness, then the third line of inquiry, the philosophy of religion, enters. Its particular function is to survey as comprehensively as possible the entire picture, to ask what is true and what is false in it all, and to set forth a reasoned conception of religious truth.

74. What Is the Philosophy of Roman Catholicism?

Of several major types of religious philosophy which prevail in contemporary Western thought, primacy belongs as far as date of formulation is concerned to the philosophy of religion held by Roman Catholicism. This philosophy was stated in its essential outlines by Thomas Aquinas, who lived from A.D. 1225 to 1274. For a long time "Neo-Platonism" had been the dominant influence philosophically speaking in the church and had led to a predominant emphasis upon mysticism and intuition. Now, however, the long-lost philosophy of Aristotle had again become known and was leading to a renewed interest in empirical observation and logical reasoning. The work of Thomas was done under the influence of Aristotle and in the spirit of rational inquiry. The result, it has been said, was that Thomas Christianized Aristotle and Aristotelianized Christian theology. At all events, what emerged was a formulation of Christian belief, so clear, logical, and impressive that it has remained the definitive philosophy of religion in the Roman Catholic Church until today.

Thomas Aquinas made a very interesting distinction between natural religion and revealed religion. He believed that one could go a certain distance by the use of the reason alone, but after this it was necessary to accept the supernatural revelation which came through the church. At least two basic points of belief could be established, he thought, by the natural reason. These are the existence of God and the reality of the soul. The existence of God could be demonstrated, Thomas believed, to anyone who was willing to think logically. In order to make this demonstration, Thomas set forth five arguments. They are known as the arguments from motion, from efficient causation, from possibility and necessity, from the gradation found in things, and from the governance of the world. The general nature of the reasoning may be seen, for example, in the second argument, namely that from efficient causation. The essential point is that all created things imply a Creator. Like a sculptor and his clay or a mind and its idea, a cause must always be equally or more inclusive and enduring than its effect. In the words of Thomas, himself: "There is no case known (neither is it, indeed, possible) in which a thing is found to be the efficient cause of itself; for so it would be prior to itself, which is impossible. . . . Therefore, it is necessary to put forward a First Efficient Cause, to which everyone gives the name of God." By this and the other arguments, Thomas establishes the existence of God as the unchangeable, primary, necessary, perfect, and intelligent Cause of all things. Then by similar arguments he proceeds to prove the reality and also the spirituality, freedom, and immortality of the human soul. The lines of reasoning followed by Thomas are very rigorous and often seem convincing even today insofar as it is possible to obtain conviction by such methods.

Having proceeded this far, however, he turns from natural religion to revealed religion. When we know about the existence of God and the reality of the soul, we are brought to realize our need for salvation. When we look about for this salvation, we see the Roman Catholic Church standing there, adequate, according to Thomas, to meet all our spiritual needs and longings. We have only to surrender ourselves to this Church, Thomas taught, in order to receive through its sacraments the salvation we seek.

75. What Is the Fundamentalist Philosophy of Religion?

The Roman Catholic philosophy of religion comes to a climax as we have just seen with an affirmation of the indispensable efficacy of the church and its sacraments for salvation. The Protestant reformers disagreed with this. They saw that the Roman Catholic Church had in actuality grown corrupt and that its sacraments had become virtually magical practices. In the place of the church, therefore, they put the Bible. The man who sought salvation should not throw himself upon Rome but devote himself to the study of the word of God. Therein, he would find the way of faith set forth, in which by the grace of Jesus Christ he could come directly to God. This is the great essential truth of Protestantism which still appears luminous and life-giving.

The fundamentalist philosophy of religion is simply an attempt to maintain absolutely unchanged the orthodox Bible-centered position of Protestantism. In its central desire, this is both understandable and good. In its rigorous inflexibility, however, the program runs into difficulty. Protestantism taught Biblical faith and fundamentalism maintains that emphasis with altogether commendable zeal. Protestantism taught something else, however, namely liberty and freedom. The spirit of liberty and freedom was directly favorable to the growth of science. On behalf of

Biblical faith, fundamentalism characteristically opposes
science and is therefore in the sad position of contradicting
an important element in its own heritage. The belief in the
Bible, which is the central truth of the fundamentalist
philosophy of religion, is taken to mean acceptance of its
verbal inspiration and infallible authority in all fields.
This is a position which can no longer be satisfactorily
maintained and which has done a great deal of damage
to the progress of religious thought. On the other hand,
the steadfast maintenance in the fundamentalist philosophy of the central importance of Biblical faith has been
of great value.

As set forth by J. G. Machen, for example, the fundamentalist philosophy of religion runs something like this.
When we hear the preaching of the Bible, our conscience
is awakened and it tells us that we are sinners before God.
At the same time, the Bible brings us a revelation of the
forgiveness of God which is freely available. We know
that what the Bible tells us is absolutely authentic by the
response of our own moral nature to it, and also by the
miracles and the fulfillments of prophecy which are contained in it. Therefore, we accept it as our infallible guide.
When the Bible tells us of the gracious forgiveness of God
which is available in Christ, we are moved to respond by
faith, and this brings our salvation. Then, we are naturally
led to join with other believers in the church.

76. What Is Modernism?

The attitude taken toward science in the philosophy of
religion called modernism is exactly the opposite of that
in fundamentalism. The keynote of modernism is an acceptance of the spirit and findings of science and a ready
willingness to adjust religious thought as often and as

much as is necessary to bring it into harmony with science. The existence of this attitude and of the philosophy derived from it is a phenomenon chiefly limited to the Protestantism of the nineteenth and twentieth centuries. The beginnings of a modernist movement appeared at one time in Roman Catholicism but were effectively discouraged. In line with its essential nature, modernism has accepted all such things as the theory of evolution, the historical criticism of the Bible, and the scientific study of comparative religion. The changes required to bring Christian thought into harmony with the findings in these various fields are regarded as necessary as a part of the growth of Christian faith itself.

Even more significant than its adjustment to the scientific atmosphere of thought, is modernism's attempt to find the scientific basis for religious faith. It is characteristic of science, as we know, to proceed empirically, that is by observation and experiment. What is the experimental fact upon which Christian faith is based according to the modernist philosophy? To answer this question we must go back to Friedrich Schleiermacher, a German minister and theologian who lived from 1768 to 1834. Schleiermacher did not use exactly the same terms as present day modernists, but the method he pursued is exactly that which has become basic for modernist thought. In the spirit of empiricism, which he called "descriptive" method, he sought to find an observable basis of religious faith. What he discovered was "religious consciousness," or what we would more commonly call religious experience. The very essence of religion, according to Schleiermacher, is "the feeling of absolute dependence." This is the consciousness which every religious person has and which is the unshakable basis of his faith. The being with whom we are in touch in this consciousness of dependence is God.

By analysis of this inward feeling, we can arrive at the attributes of God himself. Since we are aware of dependence, we know that God is omnipotent. Since we feel a sense of sin, we are made aware of his holiness. Since we have an experience of grace, we know that he is Love. Modernism, therefore, takes this fundamental insight of Schleiermacher's and uses it as the basis of its assurance. What we know within our own religious experience is as empirically real as anything with which science deals. The importance of the Bible lies in the religious experience of past generations to which it bears testimony, and whatever in our day helps to develop religious experience, whether it be the Bible or other materials of our own time, is good and is to be used. Religious experience is to modernism a growing, developing thing, and therefore this philosophy of religion faces the future with eagerness for all that it will bring.

77. What Is Humanism?

Humanism is the logical outgrowth of modernism, according to its own proponents. As they believe, the conclusions of humanism simply represent a radical and more consistent development of the principles already implicit in modernism. It is absolutely right, humanism maintains, to accept the spirit and findings of science, and all that is wrong with modernism is that it has done this only in a half-hearted sort of way. The scientifically known universe, humanists generally say, is clearly a deterministic order which manifests no concern for human welfare. Therefore, we must accept the fact that the world was not made for man and is in its behavior quite largely beyond his control. Since the term "God" generally means a supernatural being who has made the world for man and who constantly orders it for man's welfare, many humanists draw the frank conclusion that they cannot be theists, at least in any conventional sense of the word. Religious experience, they further maintain, is really only the integration of life. Therefore, anything that integrates life is truly religious. Religion, from this point of view, may simply be defined as life lived under the influence of an integrating ideal. Such an ideal or ideals are not given us by God. Rather God is a projection of these ideals which have arisen within the human mind. Jesus taught some of these ideas but others have now come into view, humanists say, which Jesus did not know about. The whole scientific movement would be an example of this, and since Jesus lived in a prescientific age, he can only be a guide for us in a quite limited way. Real religion consists simply in the ever-advancing co-operative quest of man for the good life. The well-known Humanist Manifesto, issued by John Dewey and others in 1933, declares: "Religious humanism considers the complete realization of human personality to be the end of a man's life, and seeks its development and fulfillment in the here and now. In place of the old attitudes involved in worship and prayer, the humanist finds his religious emotions exprest in a heightened sense of personal life and in a co-operative effort to promote social well-being."

78. What Is Neo-Orthodoxy?

There is some truth in the affirmation of humanists that they have simply carried out to their logical conclusions the principles of modernism. The revelation of the end to which these principles lead is disturbing. As pictured by nontheistic, naturalistic humanism, man is a stranger in a universe to which he has no kinship. The ideals by which he tries to guide his few and faltering steps may do him some temporary good but are ultimately illusory and cannot save him from annihilation. The Bible is, of course, only a quaint collection of antiquated documents recording the pathetic experiences of a few people who were so immature as to believe in God and in whose miserable fate the fallacy of that belief can be clearly discerned.

Now all of this is simply not true. The universe is not fully described by an enumeration of its aspects which seem hostile or foreign to man; the emergence of the ideals of truth, beauty, and goodness is not so easily explained nor so inconsequential a fact as the foregoing representation makes out; and the true philosophical and religious import of the Bible is scarcely comprehended at all in the description just given. Furthermore, the humanistic quest of the good life has proved quite impotent to avert world war and world tragedy, and therefore a realization has come of the desperate need for the achievement of a profounder understanding of our historical existence, and the discovery and acceptance of a more dynamic power for human redemption.

This great need is generally recognized in our time. One attempt to meet the need may be seen in the movement known as neo-orthodoxy. As the name suggests, this philosophy discovers new values in the teachings of the past, particularly of the Bible. Karl Barth, the German theologian who had the most to do with the rise of this religious philosophy, says in the preface to his exposition of Paul's letter to the Romans that it is his purpose to wrestle with that ancient document until the wall between the first century and our century becomes translucent and the light of the truth that shone then shines through also into our times. Similarly, Reinhold Niebuhr, in such books as *Beyond Tragedy, The Nature and Destiny of Man,* and

Discerning the Signs of the Times, finds in the Bible the definitive insights which illuminate the problem of human life. The Tower of Babel, he says, for example, is a fitting symbol of every civilization and culture which pretends to have achieved finality and forgets the God who transcends its finitude. Again he points out that when the Christian community prays, "Thy kingdom come, thy will be done, on earth as it is in heaven," it shows that it believes in an actual realization of the will of God in history; but when it declares with Paul, "If in this life only we have hope in Christ, we are of all men most miserable," it makes it plain also that the Christian hope reaches out beyond history as we now know it. In a day such as ours, when there are so many wonderful possibilities almost within grasp upon earth, but when there are also so many historic frustrations, there is particular need of just this Christian gospel, with its relative-historical aspect on the one side and its final-and-absolute outlook on the other.

Neo-orthodoxy not only rediscovers a brilliant light in the ancient gospel, it also takes the problem of contemporary existence very seriously. Sören Kierkegaard, the nineteenth century Danish philosopher from whom most neo-orthodox theologians have derived so much inspiration, remarked that "existence is prior to essence." This reminds us that living has to precede thinking, and that man's profoundest perplexities and deepest needs are not in the realm of abstract thought but of actual life. When one realizes what an amazing and indeed terrifying thing it is that one is here at all, one's thoughts attain a new intensity. This is "existential" thinking, as distinguished from formal, rationalistic knowing. The importance of such an existential approach may be greatest of all in the very area of religion itself. Here it is that man not only realizes that his life is both wonderful and precarious, but also becomes

aware that he is confronted by none other than the living
God. To face God all alone is indeed the ultimate crisis,
and this is what man must do, whether he will or not,
both in life and in death. The awareness of this critical
issue of life, of this fact that in the presence of God one's
very self is at stake, is as old as the cry of the Psalmist,
"Save me, O my God," "Have mercy upon me, O Lord";
and it is as new as the contemporary writings of Emil
Brunner, who speaks of the divine-human encounter and
maintains that it is precisely at the point of the personal
meeting between man and his Maker that Christian truth
comes into being.

Pertinent as the central idea of "existentialism" seems to
be to the exposition of Biblical religion, and effectively as
it is being employed in neo-orthodoxy, it must be recognized that it is capable of other applications. It has been
made use of not only by Protestant theologians like
Kierkegaard, Barth, and Brunner, and by a Roman Catholic
writer like Martin C. D'Arcy, and a Jewish scholar like
Martin Buber, but also by philosophers like Martin Heideg-
ger and Jean-Paul Sartre, who assume the non-existence of
God and explicitly describe themselves as "atheistic ex-
istentialists." [1] Thus it can hardly be said that existentialism
in and of itself provides a sufficient clue for the elaboration
of a completely satisfying philosophy of religion. Furthermore, even within the strictly Protestant field of thought,
Karl Barth, for example, has emphasized an absolute
"otherness" of God which is scarcely defensible within the
structure of modern thought. Indeed, such an affirmation
seems to go as far to the extreme on one side as humanism went on the other. Therefore, while neo-orthodoxy
may be gratefully acknowledged to have deepened our
understanding of the Bible and heightened our sense of

---

[1] Jean-Paul Sartre, *Existentialism*, p. 15.

urgency and significance in life itself, the ultimate philosophy of religion must be held to lie yet beyond anything hitherto achieved.

For Further Reading

Edgar S. Brightman, A Philosophy of Religion. New York, Prentice-Hall, Inc., 1940.

Emil Brunner, The Divine-Human Encounter. Philadelphia, The Westminster Press, 1943.

Emil Brunner, Revelation and Reason. Philadelphia, The Westminster Press, 1946.

Martin Buber, I and Thou. Edinburgh, T. and T. Clark, 1937.

Martin Buber, Between Man and Man. New York, The Macmillan Company, 1948.

M. C. D'Arcy, The Mind and Heart of Love. New York, Henry Holt and Company, 1947.

John Dewey, A Common Faith. New Haven, Yale University Press, 1934.

Nels F. S. Ferré, Faith and Reason. New York, Harper and Brothers, 1946.

Nels F. S. Ferré, Pillars of Faith. New York, Harper and Brothers, 1947.

A. Campbell Garnett, A Realistic Philosophy of Religion. Chicago, Willett, Clark and Company, 1942.

James G. Gilkey, A Faith to Affirm. New York, The Macmillan Company, 1940.

Marjorie Grene, Dreadful Freedom, A Critique of Existentialism. Chicago, The University of Chicago Press, 1948.

Georgia Harkness, Understanding the Christian Faith. Nashville, Abingdon-Cokesbury Press, 1947.

Ralph Harper, Existentialism. Cambridge, Harvard University Press, 1948.

J. G. Machen, Christianity and Liberalism. New York, The Macmillan Company, 1923.

J. G. Machen, The Christian Faith in the Modern World. New York, The Macmillan Company, 1936.

William P. Montague, *Belief Unbound*. New Haven, Yale University Press, 1930.

Reinhold Niebuhr, *Beyond Tragedy*. New York, Charles Scribner's Sons, 1937.

Reinhold Niebuhr, *The Nature and Destiny of Man*. 2 vols. New York, Charles Scribner's Sons, 1941–43.

Reinhold Niebuhr, *Discerning the Signs of the Times*. New York, Charles Scribner's Sons, 1946.

Bertrand Russell, *Religion and Science*. New York, Henry Holt and Company, 1935.

Jean-Paul Sartre, *Existentialism*. New York, Philosophical Library, 1947.

B. H. Streeter, *Reality*. New York, The Macmillan Company, 1927.

Paul Tillich, *The Shaking of the Foundations*. New York, Charles Scribner's Sons, 1948.

D. Elton Trueblood, *The Logic of Belief*. New York, Harper and Brothers, 1942.

Henry N. Wieman, *The Source of Human Good*. Chicago, The University of Chicago Press, 1946.

PRAYER AND WORSHIP

79. Is Prayer Autosuggestion?

IT HAS been fashionable in certain circles to describe prayer as autosuggestion. Autosuggestion means self-suggestion, or giving an idea to our own minds with great force and concentration. For example, a person may get the idea that he is sick and may concentrate on that idea so hard that it actually produces a functional disturbance, or on the other hand he may suggest the idea of recovery to himself so strongly that it cures this disturbance. The theory we are now discussing supposes that this same thing is what really happens when a person prays. He may think that he is addressing himself to a supernatural deity, but that is a quite irrelevant matter. What happens is that he forces his mind to concentrate upon certain ideas and they in turn have their influences upon himself. It is therefore argued that prayer in the traditional sense might as well be abandoned and this process of psychological self-adjustment be substituted for it. As a matter of fact, one philosopher offered as his panacea for all human ills the daily repetition of the sentence, "Every day in every way I am getting better and better."

One's instinctive reaction to this theory may be to repudiate it altogether since it seems to reduce prayer to self-delusion. Possibly, however, there is at least an element of truth in it. In his book, Prayer and Worship, Douglas V. Steere asks what is the opposite of autosuggestion and answers with the word "heterosuggestion." Heterosuggestion is other-suggestion. It is all the ideas and impacts that come to us from the outside, from other persons and from our environment in general. When we stop to think about it, there are of course a multitude of such heterosuggestions being flung at us constantly. Whenever we walk down the street, the billboards and shop windows hurl at us the ideas they are trying to implant in our minds, and the voices of people and the noises of the world fall upon us constantly. We live under a barrage of heterosuggestions. If all these miscellaneous ideas are received indiscriminately, our lives will soon become a bewildering medley and a complete confusion. This then is why it is necessary and right to recognize that prayer actually is in part autosuggestion. Prayer involves the conscious and purposeful selection out of all the multitudinous impressions which come to us of those upon which we choose to focus our minds and around which we desire to build our lives. This would seem to be exactly what the apostle Paul is urging when he writes, "Finally, brethren, whatsoever things are true, whatsoever things are honorable, whatsoever things are just, whatsoever things are pure, whatsoever things are lovely, whatsoever things are of good report; if there be any virtue, and if there be any praise, think on these things."

Having then frankly and freely recognized that what is called autosuggestion has a proper place in prayer, we may go on and affirm that prayer in the Christian sense of the word is immensely more than this. Indeed, if it were not something more than this, the suspicion would persist that it was essentially self-delusion after all. If the ideas of the true and lovely things upon which we concentrate are only our fleeting, human notions which are alien to the real nature of the universe and which are made mock of by the grim reality of that universe, then we shall scarcely long continue to hold even these ideas important enough to demand our concentrated consideration. If, on the other hand, the things that are true and lovely reveal the inmost heart of reality, then we may ascend by the path they offer to God himself. Then we may advance into the full Christian understanding of prayer, which holds it to be not merely a communing of the mind with itself but a communication of finite man with his infinite Maker.

80. What Should One Ask For When One Prays?

A saying of Jesus which is found in both Matthew 21:22 and Mark 11:24 and which validates itself as an authentic saying of his by its gigantesque quality declares, "And all things, whatsoever ye shall ask in prayer, believing, ye shall receive." Does that mean what it says? Are "all things" which concern man also possible subjects of prayer to God? May we ask "whatsoever" we will when we pray?

It used to be thought, of course, that this was not right. It was confidently maintained that the universe was divided into two clearly separated parts. On the one side was everything material, on the other side everything spiritual. Material things, of course, operate according to physical laws, and consequently prayer, it was said, could not be expected to have any effect upon them whatsoever. Therefore, this theory implied, one should never pray about anything material. On the other side of the line of demarcation, continued this theory, is the realm of the spiritual. Here is where one may pray and expect something to happen. Prayer can actually influence one's state of mind and so do one a great deal of good. It is things like one's own state of mind that one should really pray about.

The theory just described does not sound as convincing now as it used to. It seems far less possible now to draw a distinct line of division through the universe and state categorically that on one side everything is material and on the other side everything is spiritual. The spiritual and the material now appear to us to flow into one another, and many times to be quite indistinguishable from each other. This is recognized, for example, in the whole new field of psychosomatic medicine, where it is seen that not only do physical conditions affect the state of the mind but also that the state of the mind actually influences and produces organic physical conditions. Other evidence that may point in the same direction is being amassed by the experiments of Professor J. B. Rhine in the laboratory of parapsychology at Duke University. This investigator believes his experiments have not only demonstrated the reality of extra-sensory perception, that is of the ability of one mind to communicate with another apart from the ordinary channels of sense, but have also indicated that the mind exercises a measurable influence upon matter itself. Beyond such specific data as are emerging in the realms of medicine and parapsychology, we may point to the general philosophical theory that the universe is really more like a thought than like a machine.

Now what does all of this mean as far as prayer is concerned? It seems to mean nothing less than that the words of Jesus may be taken literally: "All things whatsoever" we are concerned about are things properly to be brought before God in prayer. If we are really going to believe these words of Jesus, however, then we must not only notice the freedom they give us but also the conditions they impose. At least two such conditions appear in the gospels, and it may be the two are basically one and the same. The first is found in the verse which we have already quoted which states that prayer to be effective must be "believing." Prayer is conditioned by faith. The other condition is found in John 14:14: "If you ask anything in my name, I will do it." Prayer to be effective must be in the name of

Christ, which means in his spirit and attitude. This may then be essentially the same thing that is meant when faith is required. Prayer may be about any thing if it is in the spirit of Jesus. And it was the attitude of Jesus, as we remember, to say when he prayed, "Not what I will, but what thou wilt."

81. Does Prayer Change Things?

Prayer certainly changes the person himself who prays. Miss Sheila Kaye-Smith has stated this fact in these words: "The victory of prayer cannot be estimated by 'answers' received to definite petitions. If I may say so reverently, God does not advertise, and the most remarkable 'answers' to prayer will always remain hidden and unknown. The success of prayer lies not in what God gives a man, but in what he makes him; and if we could read the secret records, we should meet hundreds and thousands and indeed millions of prayers thus successful—of men and women who by prayer have been delivered from every kind of bondage of sin and fear, of leopards who have completely and wonderfully changed their spots."

Deeply religious persons also are convinced on evidence that cannot easily be put aside that prayer also accomplishes changes in the lives of other people. We have already narrated the incident reported by Dr. T. Howard Somervell, concerning the man in India whose leg was healed through the combined prayers of himself and his family and friends. Recently, that account was read from Dr. Somervell's own book in a public church meeting. Afterward, four other reports were offered by persons there present of comparable events which they had witnessed. Those who have had personal experiences of this kind cannot be convinced that prayer does not reach out and affect the lives of others besides ourselves.

Events of this kind make it possible for many thoughtful persons to believe that prayer may not only make changes in the physical lives of men, but also in the outward circumstances surrounding them. Many such "miraculous" events are recorded in Margaret Lee Runbeck's *The Great Answer*. Others are discussed by Dr. George Arthur Buttrick in his book, *Prayer*. Among the events cited in the latter book are Dr. Grenfell's experience of deliverance from the drifting ice-floe by a sudden shift of wind; the instance of the Scotch Covenanters hiding in a cave across which a spider's web was quickly woven so that when the persecuting horsemen saw it they believed that no one had recently been there and went their way; and the conviction of George Muller that his orphanage was built through the answers which came to his prayers. Dr. Buttrick concludes, as we may too, "Their testimony, 'Only prayer brought it to pass,' is too humble, too heartfelt, too freighted with conviction, and too agelong a testimony glibly to be gainsaid." [1]

In spite of this evidence, some young people may not be fully convinced that these remarkable happenings, and others like them, are due to prayer. This need not trouble them, for it is possible for one to have a satisfying and growing prayer life without complete faith in the adequacy of prayer in all respects. But at the same time he should keep an open mind.

82. Are There Various Levels in the Practice of Prayer?

The first level of prayer is often that of emergency supplication. Even a person who has never prayed may be

---

[1] P. 81. Quoted by permission of the publishers, The Abingdon-Cokesbury Press, New York.

driven to do so in time of peril. The instances of this in war time are very numerous, and in all times of disaster and danger they occur. Nor is this kind of praying to be despised. Rather it is to be honored and recognized as an instinctive and natural outcry of the human spirit. If we ourselves have never prayed perhaps it is simply because we have never yet really lived, have never yet faced life when all our security was gone and we were up against some stark and elemental threat to our very being. The prayer of emergency is genuine prayer.

The second level of prayer is that where the principle of alternation is practiced. Having seen that prayer is natural in an emergency, one realizes that it is hardly fair and right to cry to God only in such a time of peril. If we ask God for help in time of need, then we ought also to remember to thank him for blessings in time of joy. In most human lives the pendulum swings back and forth between trouble and happiness. What is proposed here is that if we instinctively pray in trouble, we should also faithfully and gratefully pray in happiness. There is also another possible meaning to the principle of alternation in prayer. We go forth into the world to work, then we return to the quiet place to pray. Having prayed and renewed our strength, we go again into the busy world of affairs. He who works without ever stopping to pray loses strength and perspective. He who prays in his retreat without ever going out into the world to labor is equally unbalanced in his way of life. The classic New Testament example of this principle of alternation is that of Jesus taking his disciples up into the Mount of Transfiguration. So wonderful is the spiritual experience enjoyed there that the disciples desire to stay. Jesus leads them down again, however, into the valley where the assembled multitude and the sick boy are waiting for their help.

The third level of prayer is suggested by the word of
Paul in I Thessalonians 5:17, "Pray without ceasing." How
is it possible to do this if one is not going to be a recluse?
Thomas R. Kelly shows in his beautiful *A Testament of
Devotion* that it can be done. He tells how it is possible
for the mind to be busily active, engaged with all the
multitudinous details of affairs, and yet at a deeper level
and in an inner retreat to be at the same time engaged in
the contemplation and adoration of God. At all times
to remember him and to live in his presence is the experience of the great saints.

83. Should One Pray Aloud or Silently, Alone or Corporately?

A very significant term is used in the opening of the
Fourth Gospel. In the Greek language in which that gospel
was written, the term is *logos*, which is customarily translated in English as word. What is a "word"? A word is
first of all an idea within the mind, and then it is the
utterance of that idea in a form in which it can be communicated to another. Speaking, then, of divine things,
John declares that the Word was with God in the beginning and then was made manifest in the actual life of Jesus
Christ. That was how the mind of God was communicated
to man in the incarnate Word. Now returning to the
matter of man's desire to communicate with God in
prayer, is it not natural that this communication should
also be in the form of the "word"? The formulation of
ideas in our mind and the expression of those ideas as actual
uttered words is a way of making known our supplica-
tions to God. The spoken word has something definite
about it. It catches our vagrant thoughts, it shapes our

inchoate feelings and presents them to God in concrete form. It is well to pray aloud.

It is also well to pray silently. To speak of that deepest level of continuous prayer as we did in the preceding section certainly implies that an inner silence of worship may exist even behind busy speech which is necessarily concerned with everyday affairs. Perhaps even in prayer we sometimes talk too much. Jesus describes some people as heaping up empty phrases in their praying and thinking that they would be heard "for their many words." Clement of Alexandria said that many people are like old shoes, all worn out but the tongue. Perhaps it is only when the babbling of our voices ceases that God's Word can get through to us. It is well to pray silently.

It is a good thing to be alone to pray. Jesus said plainly: "But when you pray, go into your room and shut the door and pray to your Father who is in secret; and your Father who sees in secret will reward you." That can be done literally by going into an actual four-walled room and closing the door so that we have privacy to pray exactly as we feel like doing, all by ourselves. Fortunately, since we are often surrounded by swirling crowds, this can also be done by entering into the inner chamber of the mind, where in a moment, in the turning of a thought we can have the privacy of prayer.

It is also a good thing to pray corporately. There is something immensely significant about standing together with other people in worship. It helps us when we realize that there are many others who are not ashamed to bow their heads in prayer and thanksgiving to God. It helps us when we join in the common repetition of words which have expressed the deepest longings of many generations of mankind or are guided by some leader whose sincere utterance directs our own thoughts. As long as man remains a social being, he will want to join with others in his search for the highest.

84. Can One Worship God Best in the Out-of-Doors?

There is no doubt about the inspiring quality of the great world of nature. The Psalms refer to the mountains and the starry heavens, and Jesus speaks of the birds and the flowers of the field. Shakespeare, likewise, penned the well-known words:

> And this our life exempt from public haunt
> Finds tongues in trees, books in the running brooks,
> Sermons in stones and good in everything.

It is well to have this attitude expressed as effectively as it was by Shakespeare's Duke in the Forest of Arden. It is certainly desirable as we walk through the world of nature not to be oblivious of the miracles by which we are surrounded and not to fail to acknowledge and thank God for all that is good and beautiful.

It is a question, however, whether one can best worship God by simply wandering in the out-of-doors. Worship at its highest seems to be something which requires discipline as well as relaxation. Perhaps an illustration from music will help to show this. Surely there is no more splendid music than the wind sighing in the pines, the waves breaking on a rocky coast, or the thunder reverberating in the mountains. Nevertheless, man does not produce great music by simply going out and listening to the wind and the waves and the thunder. Man learns only to make great music by shutting himself away in a practice chamber or in a concert hall to devote himself to the most intense concentration upon musical study and musical appreciation. Something of the same thing seems to be true in the realm of prayer and worship. Both are utterly appropriate in the temples of the groves and the sanctuaries of the hills. But for the highest disciplines of the spirit, we need also the freedom from distraction and the opportunity for concentration provided by the solitary room where a man prays alone or the church where a congregation comes together to worship God.

85. What Different Types of Worship Are There?

It should perhaps be said that there are as many different types of worship as there are separate individuals. It is right that each man should feel free to worship and pray to God in his own distinctive way. That is what freedom of religion means.

Nevertheless, looking at the whole picture across the centuries, we can safely say that at least three major types of worship have emerged in Christendom. One is the sacramental type which prevails in Roman Catholicism. In speaking of the Lord's Supper we referred to the special interpretation given it by the Roman Catholic Church. In the light of that interpretation, it is no accident that the Mass, as this renewed sacrifice of Christ is called, occupies the central place in a Roman Catholic service of worship. The altar where the miracle is performed stands at a place where every eye can be fixed upon it. The whole service climaxes in this ceremony. Despite the fact that Protestants cannot agree with the theological significance attached to the ceremony, there is no doubt that Roman Catholic worship is made concrete and arresting by its very pageantry. The teachings of the religion are acted out before the eyes of the congregation, and they too have their constant share in what goes on.

At the opposite extreme from the sacramentalism of

Roman Catholic worship is the simple silence of the traditional service of the Society of Friends. As carried out in the early days and still maintained by many groups, this service is one which requires no outward accoutrements whatsoever. A bare room is a perfectly satisfactory meeting place and there the participants sit for a long time in silence. If and when one feels moved to do so, he speaks a word, utters a prayer, or makes some other contribution. When all have done whatever they will in this way and it is the unspoken sense of the meeting that the period is at an end, they rise and go their ways.

Distinctively different from either of these two ways of worship is that most characteristic of Protestantism. As can readily be understood from the essential nature of the Protestant movement, much emphasis is placed here upon the reading of the Bible and the preaching of the gospel. This has the great advantage that it appeals to and instructs the minds of men as well as touches their emotions. It has the possible disadvantage that if the sermon is poor, the congregation may feel it has wasted its time! That shows that a Protestant congregation sometimes has the wrong point of view. We do not go to church, or should not, primarily to listen to a man but to worship God.

The tendency in these days is to recognize that men have different kinds of needs and that all the elements of ceremony, of silence, and of the spoken word have their proper part in worship. For Protestants the ceremonies can hardly be those of magical sacraments, but they can be those of simple remembrance of the Lord's death. Furthermore, both silence and speaking clearly have their place. Therefore, no single pattern of worship can claim to be the only Christian one, and at least some elements from all Christian ways of worship may be of help to us.

For Further Reading

George A. Buttrick, *Prayer*. Nashville, Abingdon-Cokesbury Press, 1942.

Georgia Harkness, *Prayer and the Common Life*. Nashville, Abingdon-Cokesbury Press, 1948.

Thomas R. Kelly, *A Testament of Devotion*. New York, Harper and Brothers, 1941.

Douglas V. Steere, *Prayer and Worship*. New York, Association Press, 1938.

Henry N. Wieman, *Methods of Private Religious Living*. New York, The Macmillan Company, 1929.

RELIGIOUS LIVING

86. Should a Religious Person Withdraw from the World?

THERE HAS always been a tendency to interpret religion in terms of withdrawal. The very word "religious" was used in the Middle Ages as a designation for one who was sequestered from secular concerns and bound by monastic vows. In other words, it applied almost exclusively to persons who were inside monasteries. It would, indeed, be a sad state of affairs if there were no religious people to be found anywhere in the world except behind the walls of withdrawal. As a matter of fact, it seems regrettable if we are driven to say that Christians out in the world are necessarily of a lower degree of Christ-likeness than those who are retired in monasteries. Going one step further, it seems undesirable even to maintain that a higher degree of sanctity attaches to clergymen than to laymen. Dr. John Oliver Nelson, director of the Commission on the Ministry of the Federal Council of Churches, declares that the term "full-time Christian service" should not be restricted to ministers, missionaries, and the like. Full-time Christian service is what every real Christian is committed to. The channel of that service may be engineering, farming, or working in a factory, but a real Christian is serving Christ all the time. If he has a church vocation and is a minister or missionary, that is glorious and wonderful, but it does not set him apart on a special level of religiosity.

The real test of the matter is doubtless to ask what kind of life Jesus himself lived. It was certainly a life of holiness and religious devotion, but it was not a life with-drawn from the haunts of men. There were people in that time who did retire. The Essenes, for example, had monas-tic communities down in the deep valley around the Dead Sea where they lived in seclusion. John the Baptist, like-wise, was to be found out in the wilderness. Public opinion took note of the sharp contrast between the way of life of John and of Jesus, and in a way often characteristic of public opinion, criticized both. Jesus described this situa-tion in the following words: "John came neither eating or drinking, and they say, 'He has a demon'; the Son of man came eating and drinking, and they say, 'Behold a glutton and a drunkard, a friend of tax collectors and sinners!' Yet wisdom is justified by her deeds." What that statement makes absolutely clear is that the life of Jesus was lived in fellowship with men and that the life of the religious person today may properly be so lived also. One feels that in this case, Jesus would regard with approval the statement of Confucius, "The Way is not far removed from men. If a man pursues a way which removes him from men, he cannot be in The Way."

87. What Is the Relation Between Religion and Service?

Religion is the inspiration of service and service is the expression of religion. We sometimes assume that the ideal of service can prevail all by itself. We argue that the doing of good is so intrinsically attractive that it is really wrong to appeal to any religious motivation to inspire it. In actual experience, however, it is again and again re-ligious faith which provides the motivating power for practical service. The last words of Baron Von Hügel were: "Christianity has taught us to care. Caring is the Christian thing. Caring is all that matters." How often it has been true that it is Christianity which has taught men to care. For a single example, we may recall the lepers of Jesus' day who were wretched and miserable outcasts, universally avoided. But of Jesus' attitude toward one such unfortunate who besought him for help we read, "And being moved with compassion, he stretched forth his hand and touched him, and saith unto him, I will; be thou made clean." The compassion which Jesus manifested on that occasion and many others, has been one of the greatest motivating forces in the world. It has communicated itself to one after another of his disciples, who from the "beloved physician" Luke to Father Damien and Albert Schweitzer have given medical service to the suffering in His name. As we read the record of the pioneering and patient service rendered by Christians in a multitude of different avenues, we are constrained to agree with the statement which someone has made, that we may as well tie roses on dead bushes and call that raising flowers as to expect permanent service unless there is a vital religious relationship such as comes to men in following Jesus Christ.

On the other hand, the fact that service is an expression of religion is clear to all. This was said most effectively long ago in the letter of James. In the time when this letter was written, some people had apparently misunderstood Paul's doctrine of justification by faith and had interpreted it to mean that if one only believes the right thing, it does not matter what one does or whether one does anything at all. James declares flatly that "Faith by itself, *if it has no works*, is dead." To enforce this point, he imagines a dialogue between two men, one of whom has the right doctrinal belief and thinks that nothing more is required, and the other who does many good deeds but makes no boast of the faith which is in his heart. The latter says to the former, "You have faith and I have works.

Show me your faith apart from your works, and I by my works will show you my faith." And James, after giving other examples and arguments, concludes, "You see that a man is justified by works and not by faith alone. . . . For as the body apart from the spirit is dead, so faith apart from works is dead." Thus it is that religion and service are truly inseparable.

88. What Is the Difference between Ethics and Morals?

Both of these words have to do with right and wrong and both are similar in etymology. The word ethics is derived from the Greek word *ethos*, which fundamentally means custom. In like manner, the word morals comes from the Latin *mores*, which also refers to custom, manner, or way of life. Since they are so closely related in their derivation, it is small wonder that these two words often cause confusion and appear indistinguishable. Indeed they may to a certain extent be used interchangeably. Nevertheless, it is possible to establish a distinction between them. The word ethics commonly is employed for the science of right conduct. The word morals may be used in the same sense, but more often is applied not to the theory but to the practice of right conduct. Thus, if we are referring to the intellectual assent which a man gives to a system of right principles, we speak of his ethics. If, on the other hand, we have in mind the acts which he does and their quality in relation to standards of right and wrong, then we properly mention his morals. The conclusion which one very naturally draws from an understanding of these two terms is that the relationship between the two things is quite analogous to what we were discussing in the preceding section. Even as religion and service are properly so interrelated that they cannot be torn apart, so too are ethics and morals. What a person believes about right and wrong naturally issues in the kind of conduct which he pursues in his daily life. Only insofar as his conduct manifests his principles can we say that he really and truly believes in them. This does not mean that one's ideals will not often reach beyond one's actual achievement in character and conduct. Nevertheless, they must always be in a living interrelationship, and it is at the very point of tension between the ideal and the actuality that we have the possibility of growth.

89. Since Morals Vary and Change So Much, How Can We Be Sure of What Is Right?

In the preceding section, we noticed that both "ethics" and "morals" are words derived from ancient terms basically meaning "custom." This fact is further emphasized in the frequent use by sociologists of the related term mores. This comes from the same Latin root as "morals" and is defined as meaning customs or folkways which are imbued with an ethical significance. The question which arises out of this is very natural. If our patterns of conduct are really just bodies of customs to which we have attached special significance because they have been practiced for some time, how can we be sure that they are really right? Furthermore, particularly as we pursue sociological investigations, we observe that these mores or customs vary a great deal from place to place and change very much from time to time. What is considered right among the aborigines of Australia may be considered wrong by us and vice versa. What was regarded as right in the Code of Hammurabi may be condemned as wrong in modern law and again the reverse may also be true. We are adrift in relativity. How can we possibly ever know what is right?

Let us begin to answer this question by frankly acknowledging that our moral standards do have a rootage in social custom. What that really means, however, is not at all that they are therefore valueless conventions but rather that they have emerged out of an empirical process of experiment and observation. In the long course of man's life on earth, he has tried all kinds of social relationships. In the relations of individuals, family members, tribal groups and larger units, almost every conceivable combination has been tried. In the organization of the family, for example, the varieties of organization which have appeared in sociological evolution include: utter non-regulation, group marriage, polygamy, polyandry, concubinage, temporary association of one man and one woman, and monogamy. If monogamy is therefore held to be the highest form of the marriage relationship, it is not because no other form has ever been tried. The study of sociology reveals an almost infinite variety of experiments in this phase of human relationships and in a great many others as well. Now the scientist commonly and properly takes the results of previous experimentation and builds thereupon for further progress. It would seem, therefore, that when monogamy, for example, emerges as the final form of the marriage relationship it may safely be accepted as that which is really right, and that further effort may be concentrated on refining and purifying it in actual practice.

That is one part of our answer to the question. Our ideas of right and wrong do grow out of the social experience of mankind. Just because they do, they are empirically grounded. They grow out of a process of experimentation which could not possibly be conducted in any single human life, a process which is as wide as the world and as old as humanity. In observing this empirical process, a second part of our answer becomes clear. There is a tendency among the participants in the experiment toward agreement in their conclusions. Groups quite separated from each other go through the long process of trial and error in human relations and come out with strangely similar results. What is probably the most striking of all illustrations of this has already come to our attention, namely, the emergence of the Golden Rule or something like it in not less than ten different religions. A few of these religions had interrelationships which could have made borrowing possible, but for the most part the formulation of the rule was achieved independently. This testifies eloquently to the convergence of social experience upon at least a few fundamental principles.

A third part of our answer may now be given. It rests upon a somewhat different kind of observation as we contemplate social evolution. This is the fact that a good many times the formulation of principles of right and wrong is due to the intuition of some great prophet. This was certainly true in the annunciation of at least a number of the forms of the Golden Rule just referred to. The principles often emerge not so much as laboriously formulated hypotheses of what might be expected to work, but as immediate insights into what is necessarily right in and of its own nature. Then, of course, the whole process of social experimentation may be considered as a testing of a validity of the intuition.

That brings us to the fourth and concluding part of our answer. If there is a convergence toward agreement in the results of the great experiment of human life on earth, and if the principles that really work are often apprehended by prophetic intuition, then the main ideas of right and wrong must correspond with something fundamental in the structure of the universe. As man's interaction with the physical universe results in the formulation of the laws of science, so too his interaction with the moral structure of reality results in the establishment of the laws of right and wrong. Among these, at least a few great principles like the Golden Rule, toward which common social experience converges and to which prophetic insight bears testimony, may be accepted as absolutes. What is needed now is not so much to question them as to try to live by them.

90. Has the Old Testament Law Been Done Away With?

The Old Testament provides a very good illustration of what we have just been talking about. It contains a large number of rules and precepts which were formulated by the Hebrew people in the course of their historical experience and in their wrestle with the moral reality of God. Many of the Old Testament prohibitions and injunctions have been shown by advancing experience to be irrelevant. Among these, for example, are the elaborate dietary prescriptions and ceremonial regulations. Even many of the Jewish people themselves are now quite ready to say that while these rules may have served a useful purpose in bygone ages, they no longer contribute significantly to human welfare and may be discarded without disloyalty to the real purposes of God. Some people who learn just this much about the matter then leap to the further conclusion that the entire Old Testament is similarly antiquated and may be safely forgotten. This, however, is not true. Just because the Old Testament does come to us out of the social experiences of the Hebrew people and out of their corporate interaction with the moral structure of the universe it contains everlastingly true precepts. From the human side, these may be called discoveries; from the divine side they may be recognized as revelations. For an example, we may refer to the Ten Commandments. Against the many ritualistic requirements contained in the Old Testament, this concise formulation of ten religious and ethical principles stands out as of special importance. Taking a single one of these precepts for illustration we find the injunction, "Thou shalt not kill." The validity of this commandment is substantiated by universal human experience. No tribe has ever condoned the willful murder of a neighbor by one of his fellows. Perhaps all we need in order to perceive the full implications of this command-ment is the recognition that all men are truly our neigh-bors. The Ten Commandments, then, provide authentic glimpses of absolute moral goals toward which humanity is striving. From the same point of view James Russell Lowell wrote:

> In vain we call old notions fudge,
>   And bend our conscience to our dealing;
> The Ten Commandments will not budge,
>   And stealing will continue stealing.

From the point of view of the New Testament there are two further things that must be said. One is that in the highest ethics consideration must be given not only to deeds but also to intentions. Jesus, therefore, in discussing the same sixth commandment which we chose for illustra-tion speaks as follows, "You have heard that it was said to the men of old, 'You shall not kill; and whoever kills shall be liable to judgment.' But I say to you that everyone who is angry with his brother shall be liable to judgment." The other point is that a person who lives by the spirit of Christ is essentially free from all law. This is a teaching which Paul emphasizes strongly. Some people interpreted it to justify libertinism, but Paul of course meant that the Christian spontaneously does more than any law requires.

As he puts it: "If you are led by the Spirit you are not under the law . . . The fruit of the Spirit is love, joy, peace, patience, kindness, goodness, faithfulness, gentleness, self-control; against such there is no law."

91. What Are the Duties of a Christian?

In the light of the foregoing we can state that it is the duty of a Christian to live by the law of love, which is an attitude that goes beyond any law. One aspect of the life of a Christian is to have this attitude toward God. The Bible teaches that we could not establish and maintain this relationship all by ourselves. With all the wrong and evil things that we have done we could not love God unless he had first loved us and shown us what his love is like in Jesus Christ. Our response certainly includes prayer, reading of God's word, and church attendance as among the practical obligations of a Christian.

In the next place it is the duty of the Christian to practice the requirements of this law of love in regard to himself. Jesus says, "You shall love your neighbor as *yourself*." This definitely shows that a right concern for oneself, one's health, efficiency, and general welfare, is a part of the responsibility of a Christian.

In the third place it is the duty of a Christian to practice this same law toward the members of his own family. Sometimes it is those nearest to us whom we treat worst. True Christianity means right relationships at home.

It is a Christian's duty in the fourth place to show love toward his neighbor. The parable of the Good Samaritan clearly indicates that our neighbor is anyone who is near and whom we can help.

It is necessary in the fifth place for a Christian to be concerned about his community. Dr. E. Stanley Jones tells about walking through the streets of a Chinese city with a Chinese gentleman. This city was described in an encyclopedia as the dirtiest in the world and its streets were indeed filthy. The shops on either side, however, were spotless and attractive. Dr. Jones asked the Chinese gentleman the reason, and he replied, "Oh, you see the shops belong to these men but the street does not belong to anybody." There are a good many areas in communities which are like that and for which no one is willing to take any responsibility. The Christian attitude, however, is one of concern which extends into the slums and all of the blighted and needy areas of a city's life.

In the sixth place a Christian's concern reaches out to his nation. Both Jesus and Paul taught the necessity of obedience to constituted authority, always with due regard to the higher authority of God. It is the duty of a Christian to take seriously the responsibility of citizenship in his nation.

Finally, in the seventh place, the Christian is constrained to seek the meaning of love in relationship to the whole world. It has been characteristic of Christianity from the very start to make men aware of wide horizons and to summon them to be witnesses of Jesus "in Jerusalem and in all Judea and Samaria and to the end of the earth." It is natural, therefore, for a Christian to work for missions and world peace.

92. What Are the Steps Necessary to Become a Christian?

In the light of the foregoing discussion it is clear that Christianity is not a legalistic system and cannot be reduced to a series of rules. This does not mean, however, that Christianity should be left as vague and tenuous a matter as it often seems to be. From this point of view there is a refreshing quality about some of the clear-cut preaching of the nineteenth century in contrast with the abstract generalizing too often characteristic in the twentieth century. Thus there was an American evangelist of the last century named Walter Scott, who simplified his answer to the question we are now considering until it could be presented in terms of a "four-finger exercise." The question which is before us he gave in the form in which it is found in Acts 16:30, "What must I do to be saved?" The answer also he expressed in words directly out of the New Testament. The first thing to do is to believe. This is found in Acts 16:31 where Paul and Silas reply to the just quoted interrogation of the Philippian jailer, "Believe in the Lord Jesus, and you will be saved, you and your household." Faith in God through Jesus Christ, an attitude of intellectual commitment and personal trust, is the first step necessary to be a Christian.

Repent is the second great word which emerges from the New Testament to point our way. It is the word which John the Baptist proclaimed in the wilderness (Matthew 3:2), which Jesus used in his own first public preaching (Mark 1:15), and with which Peter replied on the day of Pentecost to the multitude who asked, "Brethren, what shall we do?" (Acts 2:37-38). Repentance means making the necessary change of mind and life to turn away from sin and toward God and his purpose.

The third guiding word is confess. This is based upon the statement of Paul in Romans 10:9-10, "If you confess with your lips that Jesus is Lord and believe in your heart that God raised him from the dead, you will be saved. For man believes with his heart and so is justified, and he confesses with his lips and so is saved." This makes it plain that to enter the Christian life according to the full teaching of the New Testament, it is necessary not only to have the attitude of faith and repentance but also to make our stand known by an actual public affirmation.

The fourth word which indicates the fourth necessary step is to be baptized. This is found in the New Testament, for example, in Peter's full statement on the day of Pentecost, "Repent, and be baptized every one of you in the name of Jesus Christ for the forgiveness of your sins; and you shall receive the gift of the Holy Spirit." Concerning the significance of this act we have already spoken in an earlier section.

There they are then, four clear-cut words out of the New Testament presenting tangible, reasonable, and understandable steps into the Christian life: believe, repent, confess, be baptized. These are steps which any person can take and which Christianity invites every person to take.

For Further Reading

Robert E. Fitch, *Preface to Ethical Living*. New York, Association Press, 1947.

Harry Emerson Fosdick, *On Being a Real Person*. New York, Harper and Brothers, 1943.

Georgia Harkness, *Religious Living*. New York, Association Press, 1940.

E. Stanley Jones, *Abundant Living*. Nashville, Abingdon-Cokesbury Press, 1942.

C. S. Lewis, *The Problem of Pain*. New York, The Macmillan Company, 1943.

C. S. Lewis, *Christian Behaviour*. New York, The Macmillan Company, 1944.

Joshua L. Liebman, *Peace of Mind*. New York, Simon and Schuster, 1946.

Douglas V. Steere, *On Beginning from Within*. New York, Harper and Brothers, 1944.

IMMORTALITY

93. Do You Believe in the Soul?

THE IDEA of the soul is very old. It is thought by some investigators that the idea originated in the experience of dreams. We may picture a primitive man lying in his cave asleep. During the night he dreams that he is in a distant place hunting wild animals. Next morning he awakes in his same place in the cave and, remembering the dream, can only conclude that his soul journeyed afar during the night. There are other experiences which may have contributed to the rise of the same idea. The observation of the shadow which so mysteriously comes and goes with a man is thought by some to have played a part in this. It may be more likely that when primitive man saw the blood flow from a wounded enemy or noted that the breath was gone out of a deceased man, he concluded that this was the substance of life and the residence of the soul. At all events, the conception was clearly in existence from very early times that a man was not only a physical body but also some kind of a relatively immaterial essence.

The idea of the breath was influential in the selection of the actual words which were employed to designate this immaterial essence in the makeup of a man. As far as the Bible is concerned, "soul" and "spirit" are the two terms most frequently found. The word for soul is nephesh in the Hebrew language and psyche in the Greek. Both mean primarily "breath," and nephesh is so translated, for example, in Job 41:21. In other cases the same word may be rendered "living being," "life," "person," or "self." Perhaps "self" comes as near as any English word can to being a comprehensive rendering. The Hebrew word usually translated spirit is *ruah* and the corresponding Greek term is *pneuma*. Again, both of these words have as their basic meaning "breath" or "wind." For one place to show how these words are used in the Bible we may turn to I Thessalonians 5:23 where Paul prays for the Christians: "May your spirit and soul and body be kept sound and blameless." As Professor Millar Burrows points out in *An Outline of Biblical Theology*, the underlying conception of personality found in the Bible seems to be a unity of body animated by the soul (life), and with a higher nature (spirit) which may be possessed by the Spirit of God.

If some such view as the Bible presents should happen not to appear convincing to us what is the alternative? One alternative is that frequently chosen in modern thought, namely the conclusion that man is a purely physical being. There is no doubt that man's body can be analyzed into its chemical constituents and that the working of his nervous system can be described in terms of stimulus and reaction. There is considerable doubt, however, indeed there may be said to be complete confusion, on the matter of how a chemical compound can be aware of itself and of how in a stimulus-reaction cycle there can be any selectivity and free choice. Such things as these and others, however, namely self-consciousness, freedom, awareness of a world of values, and a sense of the infinite, are exactly the distinguishing marks of human personality and therefore constitute the crux of the problem. Having recognized that the highest attributes of human personality are completely inexplicable on the materialistic hypothesis, we are driven to return to the belief in the soul. Man is not only a physical creature, he is also a spiritual being. He possesses qualities which cannot be explained from the material world alone; he is properly described in his inmost being as a soul.

94. *Is There Any Empirical Evidence of Survival after Death?*

We have had frequent occasion to refer to the scientific method of empiricism, which is pursuit of truth by observation and experiment. When one asks about the soul and the possibility of its survival after death, it is natural to attempt to gain data on the matter by observation and experiment. There are two areas of investigation which have at least some bearing on the matter. The first is that of parapsychology, to which reference has already been made. Psychological occurrences of a nature hitherto inexplicable are explored. It is claimed, by investigators like Professor J. B. Rhine, that the mind is at least occasionally able to gain information through other than the normal channels of sense perception. This faculty is now commonly called extra-sensory perception and includes both telepathy and clairvoyance. The existence of this power of the mind is attested by a large number of experiments of which the results are difficult to explain fully by chance. The same sort of thing has been observed by a great number of scattered people. For a single impressive example, we may recall when Sir Hubert Wilkins was flying over the Arctic Ocean and by pre-arrangement an experimenter in New York City was recording his impressions of what happened. Detailed notations on occurrences, later confirmed when the explorer returned, included awareness of a fire on the ground, of engine trouble in the air, of icing on the wings, and of low circling of the plane over an icy waste correctly identified as to its geographical location. It cannot yet be affirmed that psychologists in general are agreed either upon the actuality of these occurrences or upon their explanation. If data of this sort continue to accumulate and are accepted as conclusive proof that the mind is, upon occasion, capable of functioning without limitation of space and time, it will not necessarily prove the immortality of the self but it will at least point in the direction of that possibility. To the person of modern scientific training, probably the greatest difficulty in the way of belief in immortality is the inability to conceive how the self can exist apart from the physical organism in which it is now at home. If scientific evidence is already available of the ability of the mind to transcend, at least sometimes, the limits of the physical, this is certainly confirmatory of the possibility of survival beyond death. In *The Reach of the Mind* Professor Rhine affirms that extra-sensory research has given a "positive suggestion" in favor of such survival.

The second area of investigation has been called spiritualism. Here the effort is made by actual experiment to communicate with or receive communications from the spirits of the deceased. As Frederic W. H. Myers says in the introduction to his *Human Personality and Its Survival of Bodily Death*, "If in truth souls departed call to us, it is to them that we shall listen most of all." Unfortunately, the investigations in this realm have not always been conducted in a truly scientific spirit, and Houdini, for example, after extensive studies declared, "Everything which I have investigated up to the present time has been the result of deluded brains or those which were too actively willing to believe . . . Nothing I have read concerning the so-called spiritualistic phenomena has impressed me as being genuine." The most that can be said at this time, there-

fore, is that scientific investigation is welcome in any field
and that if ever authentic results are attained in this area,
they should be made known to the world in the interest of
science.

95. Is the Nature of the Self Such That Immortality Is Probable?

As far as scientific evidence is concerned, at least some
data are beginning to appear which suggest that there is
something about a person which is capable of functioning
beyond the limitations of the physical body and therefore
is potentially capable of survival beyond death. What is the
situation when the same problem is approached from the
philosophical point of view? Here we come upon the perfectly familiar yet strangely mysterious fact of self-transcend-
ence. The self is able to observe itself, judge itself, guide and
shape itself. With this profound fact William Ernest Hocking has dealt in his book, *Thoughts on Death and Life*. He
analyzes the self as possessing two aspects, one of which he
calls the "excursive" self, and the other the "reflective"
self. The excursive self is a personality as it goes out into
the affairs of the world, mingles with people, has posses-
sions, and attains knowledge. In these forays into affairs,
the excursive self proceeds from a center, however, and
again and again reports back to that center. There, behind
the scenes, the reflective self is that which initiates these
activities, subjects them to critical examination, and guides
them toward planned goals. The excursive self is therefore fluctuating, temporal, and limited, but the reflective
self possesses a relative stability, continuity, and tran-
scendence which enable it to play a creative role. The
excursive self comes sooner or later to an end. It is the
self which the world knows, and which at death is a

finished thing, a life as it is known in the fabric of history. But the realization that all the while the self within has been busied with the making of this self without, raises the strong surmise that in another world it may go on in its creative activity. Death may therefore mean for the reflective self, Professor Hocking concludes, not at all the end, but rather "the gong of passage" from a limited apprenticeship in creative work to the expanded possibilities of a vaster canvas and a freer exercise of a more mature art.

96. What Is the Moral Argument for Immortality?

The empirical and philosophical approaches which we have sketched thus far make immortality seem possible; the moral argument is that it is not only possible but that it also *ought* to be. As quotations we will shortly give show, this line of reasoning was followed by such eminent thinkers as Plato and Kant.

The moral argument has two chief aspects. The first lies in the recognition that justice demands immortality. In this life there are all kinds of inequalities and terrible wrongs. The evils of life do not fall upon those who appear to deserve them and leave untouched those who are righteous. In Thornton Wilder's *The Bridge of San Luis Rey*, Brother Juniper undertook to make a tabulation on this matter from the point of view that God rewards men in this life according to their just deserts. A pestilence visited Brother Juniper's village and he drew up a diagram of the characteristics of fifteen victims and fifteen survivors, rating them for such items as goodness, piety, and usefulness. When he added up the total for the victims and compared it with the total for the survivors, his figures showed that the dead were five times more worth saving than those who had lived through the pestilence. This unexpected result caused Brother Juniper great distress of mind, and while we ourselves may not go at the matter in the same manner or with the same presuppositions as he, we too cannot escape an overwhelming impression of the terrible inequities of human life.

Is this then the final outcome of things in our universe? Is the outward fortune or misfortune which attends a man in this life the final word? When a ruthless dictator flourishes in his cruelty and a great saint perishes in his dungeon, is that the end of the matter? Is it right that things should come out like that? In the face of such circumstances, the belief in immortality arises as a demand that righteousness shall prevail in the universe, that at long last there shall be some recompense and some reward commensurate with justice, with compassion and with mercy. This side of the matter was set forth by Plato in the following words: "In the case of the just man, we must assume that, whether poverty be his lot, or sickness, or any other reputed evil, all will work for his final advantage, either in this life or in the next. For unquestionably, the gods can never neglect a man who determines to strive earnestly to become just, and by the practice of virtue to grow as much like God as man is permitted to do."

The other aspect of the problem as considered from the moral point of view is this. The moral life constitutes a long endeavor to attain goodness. It is oriented toward ideals and these ideals have an infinite quality which makes them ever recede from our grasp, ever surpass our reach. Are we then being deceived in our idealism? Or is the universe the kind of place where these ideals do not at last make mock of us? We struggle up the steep slope of moral life and are cut down by death before attaining the summit. Is that the end? Or is there an opportunity beyond death to come closer to those gleaming high peaks which have been glimpsed already in this life? Kant pursues this line of reasoning and arrives at the affirmative conclusion, "The highest good is . . . practically possible, only if we presuppose the immortality of the soul." Such in essential outline are the strong grounds for belief in immortality which are found in a consideration of the moral nature of the universe.

97. Did Jesus Teach That There Is Life after Death?

In Jesus' time as in our own, there was a division of opinion about life after death. Not a great deal is said about it in the Old Testament until we come to the plaintive question of Job, "If a man die, shall he live again?" and the splendid affirmation of Daniel, "And many of them that sleep in the dust of the earth shall awake . . . And they that are wise shall shine as the brightness of the firmament; and they that turn many to righteousness, as the stars forever and ever." Since this explicit doctrine of the resurrection did not appear until rather late in the Old Testament it may be that those who refused to accept it felt that they were the true conservatives who were maintaining the old beliefs. At any rate we know that in the first century the Sadducees denied the resurrection and the Pharisees believed in it. This question on which there was sharp difference of contemporary opinion was brought to Jesus for an answer. As we are told in the twelfth chapter of the Gospel according to Mark and the parallel passages in Matthew and Luke, the inquiry was made by the Sadducees who naturally presented the matter in the most unfavorable light possible. They cited a case which could actually have happened under Jewish law where a woman had been married to seven brothers, one after another, all of whom had died. The Sadducees, intending to make survival after death appear ridiculous, asked, "In the resurrection, whose wife will she be?" Jesus answered by pointing out that they were making a great mistake in supposing that conditions in the next life would simply be a replica of those here. It does not seem necessary to take his words as meaning that there will be no personal relationships whatsoever in the after life since it is in these relationships that some of the highest values known on earth are found. What he does make clear is that the life beyond will not simply be a continuation of this one here with all of its perplexities and troubles, but will be something radically and wonderfully different. Then continuing in his reply and using the kind of argument that would be most effective with his questioners, he urged them to go back to the earliest parts of the Scriptures and see what was implied there as to the life after death. "Have you not read in the book of Moses," said Jesus, "how God said to him, 'I am the God of Abraham, and the God of Isaac, and the God of Jacob?' He is not God of the dead, but of the living; you are quite wrong." The statement cited is to be found in Exodus 3:6 and is evidently interpreted by Jesus to mean that the patriarchs of the past live even now in the presence of God. Thus with a kind of answer which was suited to the way in which the question was brought to him, Jesus clearly affirmed that there is life after death. The God whom he made known is not going to preside at the last over a lifeless universe; personality is the most precious thing he has made and it is safe in the keeping of his everlasting purpose.

98. What Is the Difference between Immortality and Resurrection?

In speaking about the life after death we commonly use these two words, immortality and resurrection. Both of these appear in the New Testament and both are therefore an authentic part of Christian thought. The background of one, however, is Greek and of the other, Hebrew.

Immortality is the Greek idea. In characteristic form, this represents the belief that man has not only a body but also a soul and that the soul is in its very nature indestructible by those forces which do destroy the body. Plato set this forth, for example, in an argument which may not be as convincing to the modern mind as was his formulation of the moral argument. He observes that the body is made up of many different elements, the mutual association of which is dissolved at death; the soul, he claims, is a simple uncompounded entity, hence is indissoluble and everlasting. While we may not reason in this fashion, we have seen cause to believe that there is something about a personality which transcends the limits of time and space and which we, too, may recognize as the immortal soul.

Resurrection is the characteristically Hebrew idea. Making no such sharp distinction between the body and the soul as the Greeks, the Hebrew thinkers anticipated a raising up of the whole person in the life beyond. This has sometimes been taken very literally to indicate a reassembling and reanimation of the elements of the physical body. This extreme literalism seems unnecessary, however, in view of the discussion of the subject in the fifteenth chapter of I Corinthians. There Paul gives expression to the strong Christian faith in the reality of the resurrection and then takes up the question which someone will ask, "How are the dead raised? With what kind of body do they come?" In brief his answer is that as we have a physical body here, so in the life beyond death we shall be endowed with a spiritual body. "If there is a physical body," he declares, "there is also a spiritual body." Concerning its nature, he uses only analogies. Even as the glory of the sun is different from the glory of the moon and as a grown plant is different from the bare kernel which was sowed in the ground, so too is the spiritual body different from and more splendid than the physical body. This seems like a logical completion of our own thought, which has already tended toward the belief that the reflective self will possess expanded creative powers in the next life and may therefore be thought of as having there a rich and full existence in a world of actual reality. Thus, the teachings of immortality and of the resurrection are complementary aspects of the Christian faith in the life everlasting.

99. What Effect Has Christianity Had on Belief about Death and Immortality?

The effect Christianity has had on belief about death and immortality can only be appreciated if we know the ideas which prevailed among large numbers of people in the world into which Christianity came. A great many funeral inscriptions have now been collected from the ancient Roman Empire, and they give us a frank glimpse of beliefs then current. Here are some actual epitaphs recovered by the archeologists: "I paid my debt to nature and have departed." "I was; I am not; I do not care." "What I have eaten and what I have drunk, that is all that belongs to me." "While I lived, I drank willingly;

drink, ye who live." "Eat, drink, play, come hither." Such
are some typical expressions of the materialism, hedonism,
and cynicism which prevailed widely. Behind it, hidden
by the flippant words, was an emptiness of life and perhaps not seldom a suppressed but profound sorrow.

That the atmosphere of the New Testament was very
different we know well. For a single example, we may
recall Paul's word to the Thessalonian Christians, "that
you may not grieve as others do who have no hope." That
the Christians actually did have an utterly different attitude from the hopeless cynicism of the epitaphs above
quoted is made unmistakable by their own funeral inscriptions. Many of these have been preserved in the
catacombs at Rome. There we read such words as the following and many others expressive of a like faith: "May his
sleep be in peace." "Thou wilt live in God." "Thou wilt
live forever." "May God refresh thy spirit." "Mayest thou
live in the Lord Jesus." That is the difference which Christianity made!

100. What Will Heaven Be Like?

If the lines of thought which we have been following
are valid, then at least certain general conclusions may be
drawn as to the nature of life after death. In the first place,
we have maintained that man has a spiritual nature which
is not wholly explained by chemistry and material facts,
and that this nature has at least a certain kinship with the
fundamental reality in the universe which is likewise
spiritual. We may believe, therefore, that after death the
spirit of man will come into closer touch with the Spirit
of God. Since God is best known to us in Jesus Christ,
that will also mean coming closer to him who is, as we
believe, already with God. Expressions of this truth in the

Bible include Revelation 21:3—"God himself will be with them"; and I John 3:2—"Beloved, we are God's children now; it does not yet appear what we shall be, but we know that when he appears we shall be like him, for we shall see him as he is."

In the second place, we have reasoned that somewhere sometime the books of life must balance out. All sorrow and suffering must some way be healed. The Bible declares that this, too, will be: "He will wipe away every tear from their eyes, and death shall be no more, neither shall there be mourning nor crying nor pain anymore, for the former things have passed away" (Revelation 21:4).

In the third place, we have noted that man strives for infinite ideals and have said that therefore there must be, beyond the frustrations of this life, further opportunity to come closer to those gleaming summits which from here are only glimpsed afar. If this is correct, then the life beyond must be not a thing of monotony and stagnation but of continued progress and achievement. To be sure, rest from labor is a part of our picture of heaven, but perhaps to "lie down for an aeon or two," as Rudyard Kipling put it, will suffice in that regard. And then "the Master of All Good Workmen shall set us to work anew!"

If, beyond these general conclusions toward which our whole discussion seems to tend, we ask for specific and detailed descriptions of the heavenly life, we must confess that this is a matter which lies beyond the bounds of human reason. In seeking for such descriptions, we turn naturally to the Revelation of John, but even there we find that the author writes with a remarkable restraint. When he speaks of heavenly things, he rarely ventures to say that they are thus and so, but only that they are *like* this or that. He takes the most beautiful things he knows on earth, the jasper and the emerald, the rainbow and the sea, and declares that what he envisions in heaven is "like" these things. They are the least inadequate comparisons he knows to employ to suggest something which is ineffably wonderful. In the same spirit Paul looks forward to "what no eye has seen, nor ear heard, nor the heart of man conceived, [namely] what God has prepared for those who love him."

For Further Reading

John Baillie, *And the Life Everlasting.* New York, Charles Scribner's Sons, 1933.

Millar Burrows, *An Outline of Biblical Theology.* Philadelphia, The Westminster Press, 1946.

William E. Hocking, *Thoughts on Death and Life.* New York, Harper and Brothers, 1937.

Frederic W. H. Myers, *Human Personality and Its Survival of Bodily Death.* New York, Longmans, Green, and Company, 1907.

J. B. Rhine, *The Reach of the Mind.* New York, William Sloane Associates, Inc., 1947.

B. H. Streeter, *Immortality.* New York, The Macmillan Company, 1922.

A. E. Taylor, *The Christian Hope of Immortality.* New York, The Macmillan Company, 1947.